Megan does it again! Buckle up and brace yourself for a wild, thrilling, life-giving ride from doubt, defeat, and anxiety to the joy, hope, and love of a God who wants what's best for you. After reading this book, you'll see your future in a whole new way.

—**BOB GOFF,** AUTHOR OF *NEW YORK TIMES* BESTSELLERS
LOVE DOES AND *EVERYBODY, ALWAYS*

Perhaps you find yourself in a season where you feel deafened to directions or lost while looking at your future. Megan detangles our confusion and reminds us of the simple truth that God has a plan for our lives—and it's GOOD. This book isn't something Megan thought about; this book is something she lived.

—**BIANCA JUAREZ OLTHOFF,** SPEAKER, CHURCH
PLANTER, AND AUTHOR OF THE BESTSELLING BOOKS
PLAY WITH FIRE AND *HOW TO HAVE YOUR LIFE NOT SUCK*

In the season before we knew of global pandemic, through Megan's pen, God was writing words that would become part of the antidote. This book is a balm of hope reminding us that we can trust a faithful God who made each of us with robust kingdom purpose to fulfill in the here and now!

—**BRIAN WURZELL,** EXECUTIVE PASTOR &
SONGWRITER, HILLSIDE COMMUNITY CHURCH, AND
PROMISE TANGEMAN-WURZELL, CEO OF GOLIVE

For a decade now Megan has been on the top of everyone's favorite speaker list, and now that same passion and humor leaps off every page of her first book. If you have ever struggled with finding God's purpose and plan for your life, Megan will launch you down that path while drawing you closer to a biblical Jesus that we desperately need more of in our culture today.

—**CHRIS BROWN,** LEAD PASTOR, NORTH
COAST CHURCH, VISTA, CA

With winsome candor, signature humor, and a profound depth of insight, Megan challenges our self-centeredness and invites us to drink deeply of God Himself. I'll tell you one thing—I will never read Jeremiah 29:11–14 the same way again! Read *Meant for Good* and be refreshed.

—**JESSIE MINASSIAN**, AUTHOR OF *UNASHAMED:*
OVERCOMING THE SINS NO GIRL WANTS TO TALK ABOUT

I'm grateful for Megan Marshman's ability to not just teach information but, ultimately, to speak directly to my heart and soul . . . especially to my doubts, fears, and anxieties. What a reminder that I'm never in isolation but that God indeed has plans for each of our lives and we can place our trust in this loving God.

—**REV. EUGENE CHO**, PRESIDENT, BREAD FOR THE
WORLD; AUTHOR OF *THOU SHALT NOT BE A JERK:*
A CHRISTIAN'S GUIDE TO ENGAGING POLITICS

Through her vivid storytelling and beautifully deep command of Scripture, my sister Megan Fate Marshman delivers a practical and fresh approach to one of the most well-known set of verses in the Bible. Readers will undoubtedly catch some of Megan's passion for trust-filled living as she inspires us to sprint after God's good plans. If you've felt good and stuck, I've got good news: *Meant for Good* is the honest and hope-filled book on purpose you've been waiting for.

—**ASHLEE EILAND**, PREACHING + FORMATION PASTOR,
MARS HILL BIBLE CHURCH; AUTHOR OF *HUMAN(KIND)*

As someone who has really struggled with anxiety, this book widened my eyes to the hope I have in Jesus. And it's not because Megan is clever and well spoken (although those things are true), but because this book left me knowing God more deeply than I did when I started. Megan doesn't attempt to give us a list of feel-good solutions. Instead she leads us straight to the heart of a good God, because He is the only One who can give us real hope and peace.

—**EMILY HAMILTON**, LEAD VOCALIST, FOR ALL SEASONS

I admire how open and descriptive Megan's examples are from her own life. *Meant for Good* allows the reader to gain a perspective of what it looks like to have a relationship with God while giving Him your complete trust.

—GYASI ZARDES, FORWARD FOR THE UNITED
STATES NATIONAL SOCCER TEAM

Megan's absolute joy in her relationship with Jesus comes through the pages of her book, inviting me to find the same kind of joy. She helps me understand God in a deeper way, but never in a way that makes Him feel far off and unapproachable. Rather, her words remind me that God is right here with me. Megan tells me I can trust God and then shows me how.

—GRETA ESKRIDGE, SPEAKER, CONNECTER,
AND AUTHOR OF *ADVENTURING TOGETHER*

Megan Fate Marshman is hands-down one of my favorite Bible teachers on the planet. In *Meant for Good*, she unleashes biblical insight after biblical insight in the most accessible, inspiring, and human way to show again and again how great God's plan is for YOU. This book is a must-read!

—STEVE CARTER, PASTOR, AUTHOR OF *THIS INVITATIONAL LIFE*

MEANT FOR GOOD

THE ADVENTURE OF TRUSTING
GOD & HIS PLANS FOR YOU

MEGAN FATE MARSHMAN

ZONDERVAN BOOKS

ZONDERVAN BOOKS

Meant for Good
Copyright © 2020 by Megan Fate Marshman

Requests for information should be addressed to:
Zondervan, *3900 Sparks Dr. SE, Grand Rapids, Michigan 49546*

Zondervan titles may be purchased in bulk for educational, business, fundraising, or sales promotional use. For information, email SpecialMarkets@Zondervan.com.

ISBN 978-0-310-35826-8 (audio)

Library of Congress Cataloging-in-Publication Data

Names: Marshman, Megan Fate, author.
Title: Meant for good: the adventure of trusting God and His plans for you / Megan Fate Marshman.
Description: Grand Rapids: Zondervan, 2020. | Includes bibliographical references. | Summary: "Meant for Good is a power-packed, biblical look at the truth that you really can trust God's plan for your life—no matter what it looks like. Dynamic teacher and storyteller Megan Fate Marshman will help you stop counting yourself out of a hopeful future, start living in active dependence on God, and find your way to God's good plan for you"—Provided by publisher.
Identifiers: LCCN 2019057653 (print) | LCCN 2019057654 (ebook) | ISBN 9780310358244 (trade paperback) | ISBN 9780310358251 (ebook)
Subjects: LCSH: God (Christianity)—Will. | Providence and government of God—Christianity.
Classification: LCC BT135 .M288 2020 (print) | LCC BT135 (ebook) | DDC 231/.5—dc23
LC record available at https://lccn.loc.gov/2019057653
LC ebook record available at https://lccn.loc.gov/2019057654

Published in association with The Bindery Agency, www.TheBinderyAgency.com.

Cover design: Brand Navigation
Interior design: Denise Froehlich

Printed in the United States of America

20 21 22 23 24 / LSC / 10 9 8 7 6 5 4 3 2 1

For my Sugar—
Sorry the nickname stuck.
I'm so in love with you.

CONTENTS

GOD'S PLAN FOR YOUR LIFE

Let me start this book with a wholehearted welcome. Gut-honest truth, I'm thrilled you're with me on this ride! I would only write this stuff down if it had changed my own life in worthwhile ways.

Here's what you can expect: in the pages of this book, you'll be deeply challenged and convicted by Jesus's example. You'll be inspired by stories both biblical and personal. And you'll be equipped with practical, life-changing truths.

In this book, we'll be studying Jeremiah 29:11–14. Yes, everyone loves Jeremiah 29:11, and we'll talk about that. But let's not forget that this favorite verse has a context and consequences. There's so much more to unpack.

Before we get into it, though, I want to tell you something. This is important. I want to share this with you as delicately and urgently as I believe God would communicate it to you Himself: *You can trust God's plans for your life.*

Maybe that statement takes you aback. Maybe it makes

you want to close the book. Maybe you're thinking, *Megan doesn't know me, or my life, and if she did, she wouldn't suggest something like that because the life I'm living doesn't feel like a plan God would write.* Well, here's the deal. If you find that hard to believe, you are in *exactly* the right place. This book will offer a way for you to come to believe those words, to embrace the unknown they offer, and to do so joyfully, amidst all the real difficulties you're facing.

You can trust God's plans even though you don't yet know what they are. You can trust them even if nothing in your life looks good. You can trust His plans for you because even though His plans may not be what you expected, they're good, because *He is good,* in ways we can only begin to understand.

When that truth settles into our hearts, we can live in trust and active dependence on Him. This book will teach you how. Plus, that kind of life is going to go way, way beyond your expectations. Don't believe me? Good. I have about two hundred pages to convince you.

Come on, my friend, we have a wonderful road ahead.

PART 1

*"For I know the plans I have for you,"
declares the Lord, "plans to prosper you
and not to harm you, plans to give you
hope and a future."*

—Jeremiah 29:11

CHAPTER 1

VOW OF SILENCE

"For I know the plans *I have for you,"*
declares the LORD, *"plans to prosper you and*
not to harm you, plans to give you hope and
a future."

• • • • •

God knows the plans, but He's not planning
to tell them to us.

When I was a professor at Azusa Pacific University, I had the honor of teaching an 8 a.m. class on Monday mornings. *Bleh.* I was more awake than the students were, but not by much. We all needed a little help to get class launched.

To warm up the classroom, I asked my students if anyone had done anything interesting over the weekend. There were typically one or two stories about hastily planned road trips, surprise birthday parties, or dorm life pranks. Every now and again, though, somebody went off the map.

"I took a vow of silence," a student boasted one Monday. He told the class how he refused to talk the entire weekend. He navigated his forty-eight hours with gestures and meaningful head nods, and, when he got desperate, he used pen and paper. He wrapped up his story and challenged me, "You should try it!"

I grinned and mouthed, *Okay.*

I'm always up for a challenge. Even at 8 a.m. on a Monday morning. At first no one believed it. After a quiet minute, the students shifted awkwardly in their seats. Another minute passed and I still didn't say anything. The room crackled with nervous energy. I heard one of the students whisper, "No, wait, she can't be serious. She's the teacher!"

I was serious. In Elvis fashion, my voice had left the building.

My students assumed, like many of us do, that in order to teach, professors need to profess. Silence was not in my job description. At first, they didn't trust me. I could see it on some of those groggy faces—this was going to be a waste of their time. They worried that my spontaneous challenge would interrupt that day's plans, that their time spent with me would be pointless because I wasn't going to play the part they expected me to play. They wanted the answers delivered nice and tidy in a PowerPoint presentation. Don't we all?

But as I stood there in front of the class, the focus of their confused expressions, I played with the realization that I could teach just as well if I *listened* and *invited* my students to trust me. We could explore the lesson in a new way, gathering answers together. I took on a new role, so my students had to take on a new role too. They would have to become the initiators. Talk about a learning experience!

One student asked, "Well, like, did anyone do the reading?"

To my chagrin, only a smattering of students raised their hands. At least they were honest. I rolled my eyes; the students chuckled.

I gestured for one of my responsible students to come to the front and set him up with my lesson slides. Shifting his feet behind the lectern, he raised an eyebrow at me.

"You sure about this?" he asked.

I gave him an encouraging nod.

"Here goes nothin'."

He clicked on the first slide and the lesson began. It was evident he had at least skimmed the reading assignment as he walked the class through what he could remember. As we went along, other students jumped in on the action. Students I had seen sleep through the class before started participating. They shared their thoughts and opinions. They disagreed politely, asking each other for evidence from the text. They even opened their textbooks in class. Imagine that!

I was no longer Professor Marshman: Purveyor of Answers; instead, I became the guide on the journey to the students' discovery. If the students were missing concepts by inches, I typed out a clue or a question on the screen for the class to see. The lesson plan for my Health and Wellness class that day was to discover what it meant to be healthy. In order to be wholly healthy, we had to consider every spiritual, emotional, mental, physical, and social part of our beings. We couldn't just focus on one. I mean, if you look good in spandex but have no friends, are you truly healthy?

My students started spouting off their thoughts and found themselves on a rabbit trail of opinions. As their opinions piled up, I would bring them back to the textbook. But I didn't give them the answers. Instead, I offered questions or pointed them back to the true expert on the subject.[1] I stepped to their side and accompanied them on their journey.

On my drive home, I couldn't help but think about how awesome that 8 a.m. class had turned out. It was a far cry from what I'd originally planned, but the students actually enjoyed it. Their engagement with the content was off the charts! For the first time in my teaching career, I had confidence that each student had grasped and discovered the day's lesson plan. They were still talking about wanting to live healthy as they walked out of class.

"God, I wish everything was taught that way. Even church!"

And then it hit me, *hard.*

Professor God

I realized that, up until that day, I had approached my relationship with God like He was the teacher and I was the student. I had a whole list of assumptions about His role and my role. My role went something like this: I went to church, sat in a pew, took out my notebook, and got ready to jot down the answers for my life's problems. Professor God's role was to give me answers, in a more or less immediate fashion. And when I didn't hear those answers packaged nicely in an entertaining and inspirational way, I felt despondent, or worse, apathetic. I felt tempted to give Professor God a bad semester review.

I think most of us assume God is the teacher at the front of the classroom. According to us, He should dish out answers and lesson plans, or rather, life plans, all tailored to our individual expectations. And when the answers don't arrive in the form we expect, or don't arrive at all, we think something is wrong with us or our teacher. But God is so much more than an answer giver. He's our guide for life's journey, the one who walks beside us—in our messes with us—helping us to see exactly what we need, when we need it.

Doling out answers and pitch-perfect plans is not God's teaching style. Instead, He's more into the Socratic method, "a cooperative dialogue between individuals, based on asking and answering questions to stimulate critical thinking and to draw out ideas and underlying presuppositions."[2] In fact, Jesus much preferred questions to answers. Here is just a sampling of the penetrating questions Jesus asked:

- Can any one of you, by worrying, add a single hour to your life? (Matthew 6:27)
- Why are you anxious? (Matthew 6:28 NAB)
- Why do you notice the splinter in your brother's eye, but do not perceive the wooden beam in your own eye? (Matthew 7:3 NAB)
- Why are you so afraid? (Matthew 8:26)
- Why do you entertain evil thoughts in your hearts? (Matthew 9:4)
- Do you believe that I am able to do this? (Matthew 9:28)
- Why did you doubt? (Matthew 14:31)
- Who do you say I am? (Matthew 16:15)
- What good will it be for someone to gain the whole world, yet forfeit their soul? (Matthew 16:26)
- What do you want me to do for you? (Matthew 20:32)

- Why are you testing me? (Matthew 22:18 NAB)
- Are your hearts hardened? Do you have eyes but fail to see, and ears but fail to hear? (Mark 8:17–18)
- What are you thinking in your hearts? (Luke 5:22 NAB)
- What good does it do for you to say I am your Lord and Master if what I teach you is not put into practice? (Luke 6:46 TPT)
- Where is your faith? (Luke 8:25)
- If even the smallest things are beyond your control, why are you anxious about the rest? (Luke 12:26 NAB)
- For who is greater: the one seated at the table or the one who serves? (Luke 22:27 NAB)
- Are you asleep? (Mark 14:37) Why are you sleeping? (Luke 22:46 NAB)
- What are you looking for? (John 1:38 NAB)
- What do you want? (John 1:38)
- Do you want to be well? (John 5:6 NAB)
- How can you believe since you accept glory from one another but do not seek the glory that comes from the only God? (John 5:44)
- Woman, where are they? Has no one condemned you? (John 8:10)
- If I am telling you the truth, why don't you believe me? (John 8:46)
- Do you realize what I have done for you? (John 13:12 NAB)
- Have I been with you for so long and you still do not know me? (John 14:9 NAB)
- Do you love me? (John 21:16)

Overall, Jesus asked 307 questions Himself, and He was asked 183 questions, and of those He answered only three questions directly.[3] The One who had the answer to every single question was less interested in giving the answers and more interested in getting people to engage with Him, listen, think, and respond. He was far more interested in relationship than dishing out answers.

Jesus is more interested in our *being* than in our *doing*. If it was just about doing, He would sit on our right shoulder all the time, whispering instructions to us. "Don't touch that. Don't go there. Smile at that person. Give that server a bigger tip. For My sake, don't even think about it!"

But Jesus wants to capture our hearts, not program our hands and feet. He wants us to *become* the kind of people who, by instinct, want to *do* the right thing. He wants our doing to flow out of a being that has been shaped by nearness to Him. He wants us to draw close to Him and learn His heart. He wants us to internalize His values, so that we might, with His help, do as He would do.

All that to say, God cares about relationship.

Seeking God, Not Answers

Now, don't get me wrong. God hasn't taken a vow of silence, like I did. He does speak to us, much more frequently than we realize. Relationship requires communication, and He wants a relationship with us. He wants us to know Him. He longs for us to unveil His mysteries and discover more about His character. He wants us to delve into this marvelous and difficult world we live in, all of its complexities in tow. God wants to collaborate with us, even though He obviously does not need our help to run the universe.

My silence with my students invited them into deeper relationship with me because it forced them to trust my nudges. My silence opened the door for them to have a deeper understanding of the material they needed to learn. In the same way, God's silence about His "lesson plan of the day" forces us into a deeper relationship with Him as we seek His will. It forces us to examine our textbook (the Bible) more carefully, and to pay attention when through His Spirit He is nudging us toward an answer. Like the student on the receiving end of a brilliant Socratic dialogue, we may be ignorant and even stupid at first, but our wise God will lead us step-by-step to an answer that we seemingly discover for ourselves.

None of this is possible, however, if we don't seek God first. And if we are seeking God, we need to read His Word, which is the primary way He speaks to us. He has given us the gift of the Bible to reveal Himself to us. As we learn about Him, we also learn about ourselves, made in His image, and about the world that He has given us.

It's vital to maintain that order when reading the Bible: God and then us. We cannot start with ourselves, or we will inevitably distort the revelation of God in the Bible. We will make Him in *our* image rather than learn to reflect *His* image. If our highest goal is to know ourselves, the Bible is the wrong book. But if we seek to know God above all, we will come to know ourselves as well.

If we read the Bible and seek to know Him first, we give up control over the outcomes and the answers. We will find, more often than not, that the answers we get are not always the answers we wanted. Because it's not about us and our limited perspectives on life, the universe, and everything in it. It's about Him: *His* perspective, *His* plan, *His* purposes.

While we want answers to life's questions from the One who has all of them (I mean, c'mon, He knows *everything*), I have a feeling He wants something else for us: relationship. We want answers and quick solutions to our problems; God wants trust.

Trusting God

If a trust in God is what God wants for us, there's got to be a good reason for it. Maybe His silence is just the invitation we need to seek Him.

What does that invitation look like for you? He may be asking you to trust Him with the unknowns, like your future. But what if you *need* to know the future? If we can't actively trust God with our future, we will never be free of our anxiety and fear. Perhaps God is inviting you to rely on His guidance in a difficult relationship. Maybe it's time to stop being content with everything being "fine" and surrender your entire life to the lordship of God.

You've probably heard this before: "When you ask God for patience, He'll give you an opportunity to exercise it." Cliché? Maybe. But it's true. Dwell on this for a minute. He doesn't just drop spiritual growth in our lap; He gives us a chance to put our faith into practice. Ironically, the difficulties we face in trusting God give us the opportunity to actually trust Him.

Is your mind spinning yet?

Which of your circumstances and challenges could be

opportunities for you to trust Him? How can you grow in your trust in Him and His plans, right where you are, right in the midst of the trial, the waiting, or the fear?

That's not a shallow invitation. I have sat in waiting rooms too. I hate that they're even called that—waiting rooms. Those rooms that exist for us to wait while wondering about God's plans for us or our loved ones. In those waiting rooms of life, God is not silent. He is declaring, "I have plans. Will you trust Me? Will you see Me in everything?"

As we go through these pages together, we'll get to know the God who asks that question. God doesn't exempt us from worry or wondering. But He provides a location for worry and wondering to exist: in relationship with Him. Every desire we have for answers about our future draws us toward the conclusion that He uses all of it to deepen our trust in Him.

I Thought This Book Was about Jeremiah 29

It is.

While Jeremiah 29:11 quotes God telling other people about His plans for them, the next three verses are His invitation to trust Him (and to see His plans and His timing).

Not only does He invite people to trust Him, He specifies how. Jeremiah 29:11–14 provides us with what we need to develop a trusting relationship with God. Each chapter in this book will break down a portion of a verse, drawing on a whole swath of biblical teaching.

To begin, though, we need some context for Jeremiah 29. So let's look at that briefly.

The book of Jeremiah preserves an account of the

prophetic ministry of Jeremiah, whose ministry began in 626 BC and ended sometime after 586 BC.[4] Here's the back story. The Jewish people disobeyed God. As a direct result of that disobedience, God sent them into exile to Babylon. Jeremiah revolves around this Babylonian exile.

In chapter 28 we meet Hananiah, who (falsely) prophesied a near future of peace for Israel, saying they'll be returning to Jerusalem within a few short years. This false prophet promised that their circumstances would get better, *and soon*. The problem was, things did not get better.

Today, we see Hananiahs all over the place, prophesying a similar message: *Everything will get better and easier with God*. No wonder people have pulled Jeremiah 29:11 out of its context. We want a hope-filled future with a dose of prosperity, but we don't want exile. We want to be faithful like Jesus, but we don't want to carry a cross. We want love without sacrifice, holiness without pain, and refinement without fire.

Jeremiah rebukes Hananiah and predicts his death in chapter 29. Yep, this is the same chapter that people use for the "hope and future" references iced on graduation cakes and pasted on greeting cards. Jeremiah goes on to tell the Israelites that their exile would continue. Relief would *eventually* come, but not quickly. In fact, it would take seventy more years. He encouraged them in the meantime to grow a family, plant vineyards, and seek the prosperity of the city they lived in.

Back to Jeremiah 29:11: "'For I know the plans I have for you,' declares the Lord . . ." Notice how Jeremiah doesn't promise us that God will tell us all His plans. He simply wrote that God knows the plans He has for us. He then goes on to describe those plans to prosper you and not to harm you. God's plans are for our good.

Sure, Jeremiah's words were written to a specific people at a specific time, but the timeless truth stands. God has plans and they're for our good. Let's pause for a definition here, because I'm not talking about the Americanized definition of good. I'm talking about the good described in Romans 8:28: "We know that in all things God works for the good of those who love him." In the next verse, Paul tells us what he means by "good": "For those God foreknew he also predestined to be conformed to the image of his Son, that he might be the firstborn among many brothers and sisters" (Romans 8:29). God's good plan for us is to form us more into the likeness of Jesus so that we can do what Jesus did.[5] The "good" God has for you is to transform you into the image of His Son so that you can partner with Him in the restoration of all things. His plans for our lives are so much bigger and better than ours.

Which of your experiences have shaped you into the likeness of Christ? Successes and victories? I didn't think so. Your formation into Christlikeness happened through trials and difficulty, right?

That's how it was for the Israelites and everyone else in God's Word, and we should expect that's how it will be for us as well. God's plan for us will include trials. God didn't rescue Noah by stopping the flood; He kept him safe in the midst of the deluge. God didn't save Daniel from the lions' den; He saved him with the beasts at his side (Daniel 6:22). He didn't save Shadrach, Meshach, and Abednego from the fire; He saved them right in the midst of the flames (Daniel 3:25). *God's plans provoke trust.*

Does our Sovereign God cause or allow suffering? This question springs from an age-old debate in Christian circles. My take is that it seems like He does both. Sometimes, He seems like a Calvinist (causing); other times, He acts like an Arminian (allowing). Which goes to show us the inadequacy of our theological systems. God defies our categories. And when our theological brilliance fails us, we are left where we started: trust.

God *uses* suffering. He redeems suffering. Don't miss that sentence. God wants to take your pain and heartache, and He wants to transform you through them. He wants to use them for His glory and for your good. Let's remember the real definition of good: you becoming more like Jesus, not only for your own sake but also for the sake of the world. Your pains are part of His plans.

How might God use the trials you're facing to make you more like Christ? How might your present hardship lead you toward further intimacy and dependence upon God? These questions will never lend themselves quick answers, but they will bring you to deeper intimacy with God Himself. *That's the plan.*

Step Up Your Game

During my (admittedly brief) vow of silence, I watched my students actively search for answers. My students had listened to my lectures for months and simply walked out of class each day with a few memorized facts for midterms. It wasn't until they took an active role that they made the subject their own. Even though I gave them no straight answers, they trusted me as their guide as they actively discovered the answers they needed. When I was grading their finals, I noticed that every student who showed up that day passed that portion of the content with a perfect score.

Jesus invites us into something truer and deeper than right answers and perfect futures. When we think He has taken a vow of silence, He's merely inviting us to step up our game as followers and pursue the class content ourselves . . . with Him as our guide.

CHAPTER 2

NOT ENOUGH IS ENOUGH

*"For I know the plans **I have for you**,"*
declares the Lord, "plans to prosper you and
not to harm you, plans to give you hope and
a future."

• • • • •

God invites us into His good plans for us not
because we're good enough, but because He is.

One Sunday I got a call from the chapel coordinator of the small Christian school I was supposed to speak at later that week. These kinds of speaking engagements are nothing new for me, but the chapel coordinator had news. A student had just died in a tragic accident.

"I'm sorry to hear that," I said in shock. I mentally rehearsed my next sentence: "I understand that you'll want to bring a different speaker, someone closer to the community, for the upcoming chapel . . ."

Her voice interrupted my thoughts. "And we have prayer-fully decided that you're the one who is supposed to speak to us."

Nervousness engulfed me, but I agreed to speak. Over the next three days at least ten crumpled messages ended up in the trash.

The night before the chapel I went to bed at 3 a.m. with nothing. A couple hundred grieving students were going to be staring at me in five hours, and nothing had come to me over the last three days. I glanced at my phone to set an alarm and noticed a voicemail from my brother-in-law. Sighing, I opened the voicemail and listened to his message:

"Megan, I heard about what you're going to do tomorrow. I can only imagine you're feeling insecure, uncomfortable, ill-equipped, uneasy . . ."

Thanks, brother, way to name it!

"I know that your messages are typically filled with cre-ativity, rousing stories, imaginative analogies, humor, and inspiring words, and this engagement will not be appropriate for that."

Yeah . . . I know.

"All I want to say is . . . good."

I felt relief washing over me as I listened to the rest of the message. He continued, "You need Jesus. You have nothing to offer them except what you yourself need in this moment—Jesus. You won't offer them humor, creative analogies, or even yourself. You have an opportunity to offer Jesus and the hope that's found in Him alone."

So that's what I did. I gave the students exactly what I needed. That morning, I gave the students Jesus. I gave them a message quietly brimming with hope, a message that would give them a shoulder to lean on rather than pat answers. I put the analogies away and told them a simple story, a story of a time Jesus cried.[1] I didn't answer their questions; I just reminded them of God's presence and that He cares about their tears (He even understands them). His presence and His heart were enough to meet these students precisely where they were.

I had nothing for those grieving students. Anything I gave to them came from a deep, active dependence and trust in someone outside of me: the One who holds all the plans.

Whenever God wants to show off His true power, He brings His followers to this place of admitting they don't have enough. He knows that's the best place to show us His rightful place in our life. When He is enough for us, His enoughness shines through us.

Feeding Thousands without Enough

What does His enoughness look like in our daily lives? Let's unpack this idea by taking a look at the story of the Feeding of the Five Thousand. It's a unique story with a motley cast of characters: Jesus, some doubt-filled disciples, a ravenous crowd, and a boy with what I always picture as a Ninja Turtle lunch box.

This story is unique in that it is the only miracle (other than Jesus's resurrection) told in all four Gospel narratives.[2] Mark and Luke refer to it as a miracle, but I like that John calls it a sign. Signs always point to something greater. Signs guide us toward a destination, but they are not the destination itself. So, if this miracle is a sign, we have to ask the question, to what does it point? Well, let's take a closer look.

We have four individual accounts of this story, so we can assemble a more complete picture of what's going on—like multiple camera angles of the same scene. Mark tells us that the disciples have just returned from mission work in the surrounding villages. Jesus had sent them out to preach the good news and heal the sick. The disciples return, telling Jesus about the amazing things they saw, and of people's hearts changing. They are exhausted but excited. But I can hear their enthusiasm wane as they tell Jesus the unfortunate news they heard on the road: Jesus's cousin, John the Baptist, has been executed.

In that place of grief and exhaustion, Jesus longs for a quiet place. Wouldn't you? Jesus was mourning, and His disciples were bone-tired, their souls worn thin. So He leads the group to the other side of the lake to rest. As they get closer to the lake, instead of a spacious shoreline, they see a massive crowd.

Mark's narrative says Jesus looks up, sees the crowd, and responds with compassion (Mark 6:34). In the midst of His own need, He saw theirs. Even though His plans were delayed, He opened His arms. Instead of an interruption, He saw lost hearts and hungry souls. Jesus never saw people as interruptions. He always stopped for the one (or in this case, the many).

How does that strike you? In your rush to get through your plans, check off items on your to-do list, or get to church in a mad dash (church!), how easily do you get irritated when you're interrupted?

When we're focused on our own agendas (the plans *I* have for *me*), we miss the absolutely extraordinary potential of God's plans (the plans *God has for us*). If we're consumed and obsessed with what *we're* up to, we'll miss out on what *Jesus* is up to. Could it be that we're missing His plans for us because we're in too much of a hurry to see those plans when He puts them in front of us?

Jesus exemplifies the perfect life. The unhurried, fully aware life. Dallas Willard had this great response once when asked if he could describe Jesus in one word. He said, "Relaxed."[3] In other words, He was never in a hurry to be anywhere other than where He was.

Seeing and Doing

Back to the five thousand: Jesus walks into the crowd amidst His *own* grief, hardship, and exhaustion, but He still saw *their* needs and did something about it.

He saw, *and* He acted.

Seeing and doing. When we start depending on Jesus, these are two of the things He changes in us. He first changes what we see. We start seeing the world through His eyes, and we see Him at work in it. Then He changes our doing, inviting us to join Him in that work.

I must admit though, I find this invitation kind of intimidating. Do you know what I want to do when I walk into a crowd of people? My first instinct is to think, *Okay, who do I know? Where will I feel most comfortable? Where do I belong?* My thoughts are consumed with me, me, me, *me*, and that's exhausting. It's easier to stay home and binge-watch Netflix and turn off any and all concerns. Jesus is calling me away from that instinctive, self-centered response. He's calling you away from it too.

As I've studied Jesus's response to the crowd, I've started changing how I see people. Rather than making a beeline for my comfort zone, I'm learning to ask, "God, who might You have me see?"

This one little question shifts my entire focus. It reminds me that I'm not the main character in the room—God is. Either we can live like we're the main character and everything—the good, the bad, the hurtful, the honorable—is all about us, or we live as if God is the main character. If God is the main character, then we get to walk into every room with a God-given purpose; we get to reflect His presence using our words, eyes, hands, and feet.

One thing you'll learn about me is that I'm not just a talker, *I'm a doer.* I'm a firm believer in full immersion—mind, body, and soul. So after I quell that urge to run to my comfort zone and instead ask God, "Who would you have me see?" I follow up that internal question with an action. When I walk into a room—whether it's church, a coffee shop, or a family gathering—I put my back against a wall because that physical act reminds me to look *out* instead of focusing inward. Then I ask these questions: "Who would you have me see?" followed by "And what would you have me do?"

The simple process of asking myself those two questions makes every interaction purposeful—with family, work colleagues, friends, and strangers on the street. It changes the way I see, what I do, and how I live.

How about you? Try it. Go into your next meeting asking,

"Lord, who would You have me see?" Go onto your next task asking, "Lord, what would You have me do?" Asking these two questions will help you to lay hold of the plans God has for you, because His plans for you are not just for you but, through you, for so many others. Maybe even five thousand "others"!

What's the Plan?

As Jesus watched the great crowd milling on the hillside, I imagine Him putting His arm around Philip and saying, "So where should we buy bread for all these people?"

John tells us that Jesus asked a question to which He already knew the answer. He already knows the details of His crazy plan for the crowd, and He also knows the details of His plan for Philip. Jesus poses His question to Philip, not because He needs the answer but to give Philip the opportunity to wrestle with it.

Philip runs some calculations in his head and concludes that it would take more than six months of salary to buy enough bread for everyone to have an appetizer, let alone a meal. Philip points out the material proof of what Jesus already knew. Not only do they not have enough, they cannot buy enough.

And I imagine Jesus nodding, "Exactly."

When we realize that we don't have enough, that we will never be enough for everything and everyone in our lives, Jesus says to us, "That's a perfect place to start."

Jesus ushered Philip into a place of dependence so he could personally rediscover His trustworthiness, power, and love. Jesus does the same thing for us. The plans God has for us involve total dependence. Even though it's uncomfortable, dependence (even desperation) is a gift. It forces us to look outside ourselves. This may be the reason Jesus often told people not to go spreading the news that He was the Messiah: He wanted people to discover the truth for themselves instead of merely agreeing with someone else's opinion.[4]

Let me repeat that idea. Jesus wants you to discover truth for yourself and not merely rely on or agree with other people's opinions or ideas. How do you approach this in church? Do you merely agree with what your pastor says, or discover *with God's help* how the truth actually sets you free? That's not to say that godly counsel isn't important. Check the book of Proverbs: godly counsel is an essential aspect of growing in wisdom (13:20). However, we need to make sure we never allow our mentors and counselors and pastors to do all the work for us. Jesus wants you to know Him directly. He's totally uninterested in being the friend of a friend.

The Little We Have

Jesus then turns to Andrew. I love Andrew's posture here because essentially, he says to Jesus, "Yeah, we don't have enough food. But this kid has a few biscuits and two small fish. It won't go far, but it's a start." Before I move on, let me highlight the absurdity of Andrew even bringing up that two small fish and some bread might be a good start to feeding *five thousand*. You have to wonder if Andrew was being sarcastic. I wish the Gospel writers included tone of voice in their descriptions of events.

On the other hand, it's possible that Andrew knew

something we overlook: Our part is simply to bring the little we have. God's work is not dependent upon the sum total of what we bring; it's not dependent on us at all. The outcome is not ours to control. As Mother Teresa so beautifully put it, "God has not called us to be successful but to be faithful."[5] Either we try to come up with enough or we start with what we have and rely on Jesus to do what only He can. And whatever His intentions might have been, that's what Andrew does.

Andrew is mentioned three times in the Gospel of John and every single time, he's bringing someone to Jesus. First, he brings Peter to join him as a disciple of Jesus. That works out pretty well. Then it was this small boy with an even smaller lunch who—*spoiler alert!*—gets to be a part of a radical and famous miracle. The third time, Andrew begins his lifelong work of bringing Gentiles to faith in Jesus. Amazing. What a cool resumé for Andrew! When God becomes enough for you, He'll show others He's enough *through* you. How incredible is it that Andrew is known for bringing people to Jesus? He knew he was not enough, but he also knew where to bring what he had. Andrew knew that his greatest qualifier was dependence.

God knows the plans He has for you. Those plans are for you not because you're good enough. You are not enough to accomplish them on your own, but He still has plans. And step one to taking hold of the plans is to realize your starting place in them. You're not enough to accomplish His plans on your own.

We can't be the perfect parent, work the perfect job, make the perfect income, be the perfect neighbor, or do all the things and love all people *perfectly*—and it's okay to own up to those imperfections. It's okay to admit we're not enough. Confessing our brokenness and becoming fully dependent on God allows us to actively trust the One who is enough. If we're not actively trusting God, the result is anxiety and fear, or self-righteousness, which is just as destructive. Overall, the result is a focus on the self, just like when we step into a crowd of people only thinking of ourselves and our own needs—blind to what God is doing. In both cases we miss out on the plans God has for and through us.

Let me clarify. In the midst of all this "not enough" talk, I'm not saying you're not worthy of love. I'm simply saying that God's love for you is not dependent upon your worthiness. That's what "unconditional" means: without condition. That's how grace works. It's only grace if we *don't* deserve it. The real wonder of this whole thing is that God loved us before we ever did anything for Him. That should be deeply comforting. His love for us is never based on our performance. Jesus died for you because He *loves* you. I know you've heard it before, but sit up and listen for a minute. Take hold of this. You are not enough to deserve heaven on your own, but you are loved enough that He knew the pain of the cross was worth it. This is the truth and this is good news. More on that later.

If our belovedness is not based on performance, we are free to acknowledge our need without fear of losing His love. Living in this truth means admitting to ourselves and to God that we can't do it all. Anytime anyone comes to the end of themselves in the Gospels, Jesus's response is, "Yes! Now invite me in because I am enough! I have what it takes."[6] He takes the little that we bring and does the miraculous with it.

Jesus takes the little boy's lunch, lifts up the loaves, and gives thanks. Then he breaks the bread and distributes it to the crowd, and everyone receives as much as they need, with leftovers to spare. As it turns out, the little boy with the lunch-box gets enough too.

This story reminds us that generosity shouldn't spark anxiety. We often worry that if we give, there won't be enough left for us. But that's not how things work in God's economy. We operate out of the law of scarcity, but God operates out of the law of abundance. When we live with open hands, there is always enough. There were twelve baskets of leftovers. Enough to feed the exhausted, burnt-out disciples. Jesus took care of them too. No one goes hungry in the presence of the King. Then, making sure there is no way anyone could miss the point, Jesus repeats the process with the fish.

Here is a beautiful foreshadowing of what Jesus, the Bread of Life, would eventually do the night of His betrayal: Pick up bread (representing himself), give thanks, break it, and distribute it to those in need. When we bring the pieces of our lives to God, Jesus takes the little we have, gives thanks for it, and distributes it to those around us. Friends, here's the point. Here's what this miraculous sign is pointing to: *Jesus is enough!*

"Will You Join Me?"

So, what might God be doing *in* you that He wants to distribute *through* you?

Although the story is commonly referred to as "The Feeding of the Five Thousand," Scripture notes that only the men were counted, not the women or children. And notice who

Jesus partnered with to perform the miracle: a young boy. The one the world counted out, Jesus invited in. This kid came to the party with barely enough lunch for himself. Yet through this little boy, everyone was fed. We don't know if everyone else knew what was going on. They were just told to sit down and then were handed a bunch of food. But the kid and the disciples knew the food came from practically nothing. One of the great truths of the gospel is that the people who offer the little they have are the ones who experience the fullest extent of the miracles.

Stop counting yourself out, because Jesus never has!

Jesus invites you to stop thinking you can do everything on your own. He wants you to step up, offer what you have, and stop trusting in yourself. Engage with Him. Place your trust in Him. Depend on Him.

God calls you—the you who doesn't think you'll be able to do it all, the not-enough you with all your insecurities—to partner with Him. When you've counted yourself out, or after you've run yourself ragged trying to do it all on your own, God reaches down to you and asks, "Will you join me? I'm up to something really good, but you're going to have to depend on me."

Hopefully, this chapter can be the voicemail in your inbox:

"I heard about what you're doing. I can only imagine that you're feeling insecure, uncomfortable, feeling ill-equipped, uneasy . . . I know that others think you're typically fine, but being merely fine is not appropriate for the things God is calling you to do and become.

"All I want to say is . . . good.

"You need Jesus. You have nothing to offer others except

what you yourself need in this very moment—Jesus. Don't waste time trying to merely offer them yourself; you're not enough. But remember, you have the opportunity to offer Jesus and the hope that is found in Him alone. Because Jesus is enough."

CHAPTER 3

TUESDAYS WITH JESUS

"For I know the plans I have for you,"
declares the Lord, *"plans to prosper you
and not to harm you, plans to give you hope
and a future."*

• • • • •

Jeremiah can discern the voice of God. Can you?

Wouldn't it be easier to hear from Jesus if He was still walking among us? I thought so too, so I spent every Tuesday with Him for six months.

If you're imagining me arm-in-arm with that white-robed, blue-sashed Sunday school Jesus, that's not quite it. I was in college, and my conversations with Jesus sometimes felt abstract and distant. So, over a cup of coffee, my friend Jessica and I decided to do something crazy. We decided to make it easier to hear from Jesus, in a self-styled experiment we called *Tuesdays with Jesus*.[1]

Every Tuesday, we pretended Jesus was physically with us. We imagined Him walking beside us, sharing a meal with us, or riding in the passenger seat. He went to class with us and to work with us; He watched whatever we watched and heard everything we said. Jessica and I met each week on Tuesday for coffee, with Jesus, of course, and shared stories about our time with Him.

I can still remember my first Tuesday with Jesus. I woke up, bright and early, and there He was in my desk chair.

"Well, hello!" I greeted Him, laughing to myself.

I felt surprised by my own confidence as I walked to my car and opened the passenger door. Because, Jesus. I took those few extra seconds to hold open His door to remind Him (and me) that I remembered. I buckled my seatbelt, grabbed my iPod (remember those?), and played a worship song, smiling in His direction, with a slow-motion point and a wink and a "This one's for You."

We drove to the coffee shop to meet Jessica. She had ordered one coffee for herself, one for me . . . and a third one. I pointed. We laughed.

"You seriously paid for that?" I playfully asked.

"Shhhhhhhhh . . . He can hear you," she whispered.

At one point in our conversation she flipped around her MacBook and we took pictures with Him to document our first day.

I didn't feel alone on Tuesdays. I put creative energy into my relationship with Jesus on Tuesdays. I talked about Jesus a lot on Tuesdays. I had to. My friends didn't find it amusing, but I had to explain why they had to sit in the back seat: "Jesus called shotgun."

I developed a new, literal meaning to the phrase "Introducing Jesus to people for the very first time." I realized that leaving Him out of my interactions was like having a person—a real, living person—standing next to me, unacknowledged.

Once, Jessica made a bed for Jesus at 1 a.m. only to wake up two hours later feeling guilty for not giving Him her bed. She slept on the ground that night. Often, I'd hold open the door for Him, and someone just far enough away thought it was for them and began to walk quicker. Most of the time I'd hold the door open for that hustling someone, but not always. Don't judge me. I'm not Jesus. I just hung out with Him ... on Tuesdays.

I listened to different music on those Tuesdays. I spoke about Him boldly and even introduced people to Him for the very first time on Tuesdays. I asked for forgiveness and quite often reminded myself that He forgave me and then murmured to myself, "That's so like Him."

But here's the reality: Jesus is kind of a strange party guest. It was true in all of the Gospel narratives,[2] and it's true now too. Once, I pulled up a chair for Jesus when I was having a friend over for dinner. I told her who the chair was for, and she looked at me like I had a third eye. The shotgun joke got old quickly, and friends would just roll their eyes and sit down in the front seat of my car. I knew the experiment was pushing me, when, sometime in the middle of the fourth month, I thought to myself, *Tuesday again? That means so much explaining.*

And then one Tuesday, I accidentally left Jesus at home.

I was at the gas station, staring off into the distance while the tank filled. The thought flitted across my mind, "It's Tuesday ..." and I remembered that I hadn't asked Jesus to come with me. The realization washed over me. Leaving Jesus in the armchair in my living room was more of a common occurrence in the rest of my week than I'd like to admit. I left Jesus at home and just about everywhere else. Sometimes I left Him in the pews at church or at a Starbucks table, or in the prayer at dinner time. I acknowledged Him where I expected to see Him . . . and where *other* people expected me to see Him. Did He belong at a gas station on a Tuesday morning? He would have gone anywhere with me, even the places He didn't seem to fit. I just didn't invite Him. Tuesdays reminded me that I needed to take Jesus with me everywhere.

Those Tuesdays with Jesus transformed me. Not only did I develop a habit of talking *about* Jesus, I became more confident talking *with Him*. What was most surprising was when I became more confident in my ability to *listen* to Him. What did He say, you ask? Well, turns out, Jesus has no tolerance for those negative thought spirals. I'd start dogging on myself for something, like being late for a meeting or distracted with my family, and He'd say, "Megan, you have a choice. You can either continue feeling guilty or be grateful for awareness." Truth is, He wasn't very sentimental about it. Or in the aftermath of a mistake, I'd consider His character and imagine Him saying something like: "You're not perfect, but you're Mine!"

The conversations went a lot like this: He'd remind me that I belonged to Him. Again and again, He affirmed my identity as His. And then He'd point me toward someone else who needed to know it too. Pretending to see Him next to me changed the way I heard from Him.

In my new awareness of His presence, I could discern His nudges. I could sense His elbows jabbing my side, making me less aware of myself and more aware of the people who needed to meet Him for the first time or needed to be reminded that He was with us. There were plenty of times when I wanted to ignore Him, and, honestly, many times when I did. But I'd look over at Him after the moment of obedience had passed, and realize that He had more chances for me, continually offering opportunities to step into His plans. Slowly but surely, I became aware of the fact that Jesus not only wants to speak, He wants to speak into every area of our lives. He wants a say in how we act, share coffee conversations, sometimes even dictate what or whom we listen to as we drive.

Tuesdays with Jesus reminded me that He is present—always. And His presence prompted me to listen.

Prophet of Doom

When someone thinks of a prophet today, they think of someone who foretells the future. Biblically, however, a prophet is a person who speaks for someone else. A "spokesman," not a clairvoyant. Simply, a biblical prophet is a person declaring the words of God. Prophets were used by God to communicate His truth.

Do you know who was really good at listening to God and declaring His words? Jeremiah. God called Jeremiah to prophesy a disruptive word to the people of Israel, to say, over and over again, "This is what the Lord declares." People weren't going to like what Jeremiah had to say. And God and Jeremiah both knew it.

When God called Jeremiah, He said, "Behold, I have put My words in your mouth. See, I have this day set you over the nations and over the kingdoms, to root out and to pull down, to destroy and to throw down, to build and to plant" (Jeremiah 1:9–10 NASB). In other words, God appointed Jeremiah to prophesy the destruction of his own nation. Wow. Anyone who tells you that God just wants to make you rich and famous and popular clearly hasn't spent enough time in Jeremiah.

God called Jeremiah to his prophetic ministry during the thirty-year reign of King Josiah. King Josiah began leading the entire nation back to right worship, away from the widespread idolatry that had been initiated by his father and grandfather. Josiah's great grandfather, King Hezekiah, had led religious reforms in Judah a century earlier, but then his father and grandfather had led the people astray with false idol worship. One step forward, two steps back. King Josiah was poised to create a spiritual revival, but he died when he was only thirty-nine (2 Chronicles 35:20–25). Everyone mourned the heavy loss. Their bold, charismatic, godly leader was gone, and there was no one of equal character to take his place. So, all of his work, his reforms, his call back to authentic worship was left unfinished.

In fact, it was worse than unfinished. The next king, Jehoahaz, kicked off a short and unimpressive group of kings, all of whom "did evil in the sight of the LORD" (2 Kings 23:32).[3] And within months, the kingdom of Judah was mired deeper in idolatry (sin) than it had ever been. Of course, one of the many problems with idolatry (as Jeremiah and the rest of the prophets point out over and over again) is that idols are absolutely worthless in a crisis (or anytime else, for that matter). The kingdom of Judah found itself in a precarious political situation, sandwiched between the Egyptian and Babylonian empires. But rather than turning to God, they tried to make political alliances (against Jeremiah's advice) with both sides, which never works out well. In fact, because of their sin, God told Jeremiah to announce Jerusalem's coming destruction by Babylonian invaders from the north.

When he declared the word of God, Jeremiah had to announce that his homeland would be struck with famine and then be taken captive. Jeremiah not only prophesied suffering, he lived through it. He witnessed the siege of Jerusalem and widespread destruction at the hands of the Babylonians. Many times Jeremiah felt like he wanted to keep his mouth shut because he knew his prophecies would make him unpopular, would make people hate him or even try to kill him. But listen to what Jeremiah said: "But if I say, 'I will not mention his word or speak anymore in his name,' his word is in my heart like a fire, a fire shut up in my bones. I am weary of holding it in; indeed, I cannot" (Jeremiah 20:9).

Jeremiah knew that he *had* to declare the word of God. He knew that an unpopular *yes* to God is always better than a popular *yes* to anyone else. But God did not call Jeremiah to this difficult task and then leave him to accomplish it on his own. God comforted Jeremiah and told him that if he would boldly speak His words and not succumb to fear, he would be given the strength he needed to withstand the persecution.

The book of Jeremiah is not all death and destruction. Many people refer to Jeremiah as "the Prophet of Doom," but the fact is he also wrote some of the most hope-filled words in the whole Bible, the verses that we are journeying through together right now. God wasn't leading His people to destruction but to repentance. Yes, Jeremiah foretold the destruction of Jerusalem, but he also urged the people to return to God. He told them God would protect them through their exile in Babylon (Jeremiah 29:5–7), that He would cause them to return to Judah after seventy years, that He had a hope and a future for them. Because he faithfully proclaimed God's words, Jeremiah got to look past the distressing scenes of his present situation and see the redeeming heart of God, the hope of a glorious future when God's people would return home from the land of the enemy (Jeremiah 29:14).

How to Listen to God

While we're not all called to be prophets, we're all called to listen to God and obey Him. Due to their many sins, Israel had a hard time hearing from God, especially when the message wasn't to their liking. But Jeremiah listened to God. God came to Jeremiah multiple times with specific instructions on what to do. God asked Jeremiah to deliver warnings of destruction to the Israelites because of their disobedience. Jeremiah obeyed and God spoke again, telling him while he was in prison to purchase land, land he would never get to enjoy. While it was seemingly illogical, Jeremiah obeyed and God spoke again, telling Jeremiah to deliver another disturbing message to Zedekiah, the king of Judah, informing him that he would not escape the king of Babylon. The directives from God were not easy to obey. Want to hear from God more often? Obey His nudges immediately! Most of what God is asking us to do will bring us far beyond our comfort zone, but God has heavy and hopeful truth that we, or others, need to hear. We may miss His words if we're distracted or disobedient the first time around.

In his writings, Jeremiah uses the phrase, "declares the LORD" 170 times! That means there were at least 170 times that Jeremiah heard God's voice so clearly he was able to tell the people: "Listen to me. Here's what the Lord says!" Let me ask the obvious question: how on earth could he have been sure? Maybe you've been longing to hear from God, and you feel like it's never happened to you. Well, let me give you one more piece of insight about the prophet's posture. Jeremiah's ability to hear God had one big prerequisite: Jeremiah's willingness to listen.

We've all done it, right? You're engaging in a conversation like you mean it. Maybe you're talking to your mom, or a friend, or a total stranger, but the gist is the same. You say something profound, like you always do, and then you start taking in the response from across the table. But then, so-and-so goes on and on about something-or-other, and pretty soon you find yourself thinking about all of the stuff you've got to do that day or what you're going to eat for lunch or why 7-Elevens have locks on the doors if they're open 24/7. After a while, if you're anything like me, you stop listening. Why? Because listening is hard, like math.

Listening is tough because it's sacrificial. It's tough because it's others-centered. It's tough because it requires patience. It's hard enough for us to imagine listening perfectly because then that wouldn't leave us adequate time to prepare our responses. We start composing our next thought while they're talking, and we're no longer listening. Now, we're just waiting for them to finish so we can share our brilliant insight. *Hurry.* You're not rude enough to say "Hurry" out loud. Of course not. You merely think it, until a second thought comes to mind. Yes! But, wait, what was that first thing again? Yep, still not listening. And, before you know it, you've had a whole conversation with someone without really hearing a word they said. Most of us are just not very good at listening.

Now, if we find it that difficult to listen to someone who we can see sitting right in front of us, is it any wonder that we have a hard time hearing from God? The problem, of course, is not that God's not speaking. He is a good Father, and He knows that the key to any good relationship is communication. He loves to speak to us. The problem is that we're not listening.

No wonder it's tough to relate to Jeremiah when he writes the phrase "declares the LORD" with absolute confidence. Check in here. I mean it, dig deep for a minute. Are you listening to God? Or are you waiting for your turn to talk?

God Speaks

Now you might be thinking, "Well, it would be a lot easier to listen to God if He was sitting right in front of me, or at the very least if I could hear His voice audibly. How do I even know if what I think I'm hearing is from God?" It's all well and good to say that we need to listen to God, but how do we know what we're supposed to be listening for?

Okay, here's some hard truth for you. Listening to God is not complicated. It just isn't easy. It's not easy because our ears are not attuned to His voice. It's not rocket science or some inscrutable process accessible only to the most spiritually adept, but in a world where there are so many competing voices and people who are easily distracted, it's difficult for us to hear from God.

You probably know how to do some things that people, on the whole, have to learn how to do: for example, swimming, riding a bike, reading . . . How do you know how to do these things? You've practiced them. If you've spent your whole life swimming, you're better at it than someone who's never seen water. If listening to God is sounding like this totally foreign concept to you, consider for a minute that maybe you just don't have a lot of practice. Maybe you've never even seen water. Breathe. That's okay. There are a lot of voices competing for your mind—and you are not alone in that. You're in the right place, and you can always start listening for God's voice now—right now. I mean, put the book down if this is your moment.

I'm trying to practice listening to God in my own life—and again, it's pretty uncomplicated, but it isn't easy. Here's an example from my own experience. Whenever I'm trying to discern whose voice it is that I'm hearing in my head (which is how God often speaks), for me I try to remember one thing: glory. Let me show you what I mean by that. Imagine this scenario.

You notice someone sitting alone. You sense that nudge to initiate a conversation with that lonely person. Whose voice is telling you to do that? Good question.

Let's say in this scenario, you're at a party with lots of familiar faces. When you sense the nudge to sit next to the lonely stranger, your first thought is, *Who might notice my Good Samaritan character? Is so-and-so here? Would they see me?* It's more about you than about that lonely person. It's very likely not about God's glory.

Let's rewind and try again.

You sense the nudge to go sit with that person. You consider their well-being. You wonder why they're alone. You are unaware of who might see or be impressed with you (including that lonely person). You simply feel the nudge to care or, even more important, the nudge that you need to obey the nudge. It's not about you right now. Who can be glorified when it's not about you? God can.

The journey of learning to hear from God involves time, discipline, and intimacy. Another good litmus test for discerning the voice of God is asking, "Is what I'm hearing consistent with the character of God?" The only way to know God's character is to spend time with Him in His Word. In other words, if you want to discern God's voice, ask yourself if what you're hearing sounds/feels like something God would say. Is it loving? Restorative? Gracious and invitational? Answering these questions with discernment requires relationship.

Another nuance to hearing from God is found in community. Smaller decisions often can be handled just between God and me. But when it comes to bigger decisions and wanting to hear from God, submit your discernment process to a community. Invite other people who you know have a relationship with God to help discern His leading with you.

Does God speak directly to people? I do think so, but I also think He waits for who is listening for His sake, for His glory, and for His purposes. For the sake of His glory, He's speaking to us all the time. But His words don't always sound like speech. God uses our imagination, He uses a nudge, He uses our eyes to recognize needs around us, He uses our mind to rationally discern a course of action, and He uses community to confirm and verify His message.

I've found that the more I acknowledge God in conversations and surrender my will to His agenda, the more I hear from Him. When sitting with a friend who is sharing a very challenging story and requesting advice, I ask God for wisdom *during the conversation*. I quietly pray, "Help! Bring wisdom to my head as I listen with my ears and heart." Then I attempt to listen beyond the words and into the experience. The reason I'm confident God is speaking to me is because in the midst of the conversation I'm releasing the burden of trying to fix that friend by myself. This takes conscious effort. It also takes a past of experiencing God's power and ability to fix me in my own life and wanting the same powerful experience for a friend. In the moment, I've far too often sat face-to-face and offered some (well-intended) advice without acknowledging the existence of God at all. What a miss. When you feel out of your depth, remember you're not alone. Embrace the relationship.

Hearing from God *for yourself* is key to your relationship with Him. When you were a child, you heard the voice of God from your parents, who taught you right and wrong. In the same way, God's Word teaches you right from wrong. But as the book of Hebrews mentions, that may be merely the "milk" of what God is trying to say. If you want to get to the "meat," you need to train yourself constantly to distinguish good from evil—to know what to do even in the most difficult situations (see Hebrews 5:11–14). You can't be lax here. As the writer of Hebrews says, "I'd teach you more, but you don't even try to understand!" Or as Yoda might put it, "Do. Or do not. There is no try."

The Bible gives us a lot of wisdom on how to hear from God. Read and study His Word, confess your sins, get away from crowds, close your door and pray, meet with other believers—all are parts of the effort required to hear from Him.[4] There's no guarantee you will hear from God, but we must make the effort to draw near to Him in the same way He made the effort to draw near to us. Relationships go both ways.

Ever wonder what God's will is for your life? It's an amazing wish until we realize the implications. Do you *really* want to know what time He'd have you wake up? Do you *really* want to know whom He would have you talk to? Or who He'd *really* have you forgive?

Do you *really* want to know what He has to say? You'll have to listen to what He says and follow it to the letter. And your obedience will bring Him glory. And His being glorified will bring you satisfaction. But remember, the success of your obedience is not determined by the outcome.

Let's say that stranger from our scenario above completely blows you off—after you discerned that the nudge was truly from God, that it wasn't about your glory. Well, you sat down, didn't you? Living successfully *is* living obediently. The outcomes are up to Him. I promise, we'll get back to this in other chapters. But for now, remember this: One of the gifts of hearing God's voice is the opportunity to obey.

Two Questions

There was a season of life when my quiet time with God involved a simple reflection on whatever Scripture I was reading. Just two questions: What do you think God is trying to tell you? What are you going to do about it?

Turn to His Word. Think about your life. What do you think God is trying to tell you? Wait for it. Think about His glory. Listen. And once something comes to mind, if you're up for an adventure, answer the next question: What are you going to do about it? I can tell you one thing I've learned since college—Jesus wants every day of your week. No matter what you hear from Him, the adventure is bigger than just Tuesdays.

CHAPTER 4

DON'T STOP DREAMING

"For I know the plans I have for you,"
declares the Lord, "plans to prosper you and
not to harm you, **plans to give you hope and**
a future.*"*

. . . . .

Your hope and future dictate how you live in
the now.

I was in an important room for an important meeting with very important people. I was made aware of all this importance when we were instructed to go around and share resumés, proving why each of us deserved to be in the room. Of course, the leader of the meeting didn't say it so bluntly, but it was obvious everyone understood the prompt based on their responses.

The guy to my right went first: "I worked at so-and-so-big-name-company for nineteen years and have done some pretty-big-named-things with even bigger-named-people."

The lady to his right went next. (This meant that I would go last. *Rats.*) She let us know that she used to be a nobody but was recently promoted to a somebody.

Each introduction sounded more important than the previous. Finally, it was my turn. I kept racking my brain for something impressive. If it came down to credentials, I should have been the one serving these people the coffee. The irony here was that these people were gathered because they wanted to work with me on an important project. Oh goodness. They believed in me and had hope that we could do something profound together. So I quietly asked the Lord what to do.

He gently reminded me of one story. *That one?* I asked Him. *Are you sure?* God nodded.

The circle of eyes looked at me, waiting for my introduction. And I said, "I went to jail once."

Jaws literally dropped.

Yep. Once upon a time, the double whammy of people pleasing and shoplifting got me in trouble. Big trouble. I gave the room an abbreviated version of that story, ending my introduction with this truth: When I put my hope in myself, my accomplishments, my importance, I find myself disappointed . . . or worse, behind bars.

I'd rather find my hope somewhere else. Or should I say, in some*one* else. But friends, I don't want to tell you in a cliché way to "Put your hope in the Lord"—I want you to know my story, warts and all. I too have tried to place my hope in myself, and I too have let myself down. I too have lived hopeless. Once you know that about me, I want to give you the good news. There is another option, one that will not disappoint. There's a deep hope that's real, that's life-changing, that brings us a renewed sense of purpose.

What Is Hope, *Really*?

Jeremiah told us that God's plans are not meant to harm but to give a hope and a future. God is not simply being redundant here. *Hope* and *future* are related but distinct from one another. Hope is a vision of the future given to you in the present. And future is, well, that future fully realized. And why is it important that God give us both? Why doesn't He just give us a future? Well, because the future is no good to us in the present, but hope is. Hope sustains us here, in the middle of a dark present, by giving us a compelling vision of the future. As Helen Keller said, "Nothing can be done without hope."[1] Hope keeps us walking forward.

But what is hope? The biblical definition of hope is different than the colloquial definition. When you say something like, "I sure hope this happens" you frame hope as an uncertainty. Hope means that it sounds great, but it's unlikely.

Biblical hope, on the other hand, is a *certainty* about something that has not happened yet. We're talking about fail-proof. To emphasize that, let's take it back to the original language. The Hebrew word for *hope* is *tikvah*. It comes from the root *qaveh*, which means to tie or bind. The Hebrew word that means "rope" comes from this same root. The idea here is that hope is a rope that binds us to a solid object. This is what the writer of Hebrews is getting at in Hebrews 6:19, which says, "We have this hope as an anchor for the soul, firm and secure." We know the end of the story, that the end is love and restoration and victory.

How you live now is determined by your hope of what is to come. If you hope you'll go to college, during high school you'll put in the work necessary to get there. If you hope that Gregory Alan Isakov is as good live as he is on a recording, you'll buy tickets for the show. If you hope that she's going to marry you, you'll lay down some cash for a ring. Hope means concrete action. Confident hope in a good future is essential to living the life God intended for you to live. And isn't that what we want? To #liveyourbestlife?

If we limit ourselves to our flimsy definition of hope, you'll be left with hoping for the Cubs to win the World Series or hoping you'll make it to the gas station even though you've been driving with the empty light on for far too long. Both would be pretty fantastic, but you better not bet on them. Far too many people find themselves living in insecurity because their hope is unsure. They're left waiting on "what ifs." So many people are drowning in anxiety because they're not practicing real hope.

He Had a Dream

Biblical hope offers the exact opposite of anxiety: a secure future. If our future is secure, we have a new perspective on and approach to the present. Instead of using the present to attempt to control an uncertain future, we are free to engage the present. Hope transforms the present. It engages each of our minutes with purpose.

You're probably familiar with Dr. Martin Luther King Jr.'s

"I Have a Dream" speech. Decades later, his words still compel us, still stir us, still call up hope in us—*real* hope, that is. Dr. King's envisioned future was not flimsy. It wasn't based on unwarranted hopes. While living in an uncertain and often violent present, Dr. King drew upon kingdom promises for the future, feeding himself and his ministry on an assured vision of reconciliation, justice, mercy, and love. From that hope-filled foundation, Dr. King declared his dream of a future that could be possible if we lived lives that were shaped by that secure hope:

> I have a dream today!
>
> I have a dream that one day every valley shall be exalted, every hill and mountain shall be made low, the rough places will be made plain, and the crooked places will be made straight; and the glory of the Lord shall be revealed and all flesh shall see it together.[2]

Dr. King was referencing the future hope of God coming back and bringing the kingdom, full of justice and mercy. He was referencing Isaiah 40.

The book of Isaiah contains some of the most remarkable prophecies about Christ in the Old Testament. For example, Isaiah foretold the mission of John the Baptist, to prepare the way for the Lord and to "make straight in the desert a highway for our God" (Isaiah 40:3). He declared that "every valley shall be raised up, every mountain and hill made low; the rough ground shall become level, the rugged places a plain. And the glory of the LORD will be revealed" (Isaiah 40:4). Sound familiar?

Later in the chapter, Isaiah brings more hope to his readers. Even though people grow tired and weary, and they stumble and fall, "Those who hope in the LORD will renew their strength. They will soar on wings like eagles; they will run and not grow weary, they will walk and not be faint" (Isaiah 40:31). Hope, according to Isaiah, was not *just* a secure (and strong) future, it was security in a person—the Lord. Our hope is not simply rooted in a future but in a relationship. We can have hope because we know the character and power of the One who holds the future.

In his speech, Dr. King explicitly says, "This is our hope," and then describes what comes to pass when we have hope in the Lord and not in circumstances: "With this faith we will be able to hew out of the mountain of despair a stone of hope." Dr. King found hope in the promises and person of Christ. Notice though, Dr. King *does* talk about circumstances. His biblical hope (confidence in what will come) informs his hopes (desires for the future), which inform his actions in the present. Dr. King's hopes and dreams, therefore, are not merely inspirational, they're biblical. While hope may not immediately alter our circumstances, having hope alters us.

And with a biblical foundation of hope, Dr. Martin Luther King Jr. dreams:

> We cannot be satisfied as long as the Negro in Mississippi cannot vote and the Negro in New York believes he has nothing for which to vote. No, no ... we will not be satisfied until justice rolls down like waters and righteousness like a mighty stream.

There he goes again, referencing Scripture, Amos 5:24 this time: "But let justice roll on like a river, righteousness like a never-failing stream!" Dr. King gets specific with what the future could look like when his secure hope breaks into his broken context. We can do the same. This is the power of hope.

God's promise for reconciliation broke into Dr. King's dreams, and the result was a specific picture of what was possible for tomorrow.

Let me ask you: How might these promises break into the messy realities you're facing today? Does God's promise of a future without fear invade your anxiety? How might God's promise of reconciliation invade your broken friendships? I can tell you this, if you let Him, God's promises for the future can invade your dreams and paint pictures of purpose for your life. You too can have a dream.

We Have Stopped Dreaming

I've spoken a few times for a wonderful organization called Student Leadership University (SLU).[3] This organization creates summer programs for high schoolers to become mature, Christian leaders. The organizational structure is brilliant. The students don't sit on carpet squares or play rec games. Instead, they learn lessons on fear near shark tanks at Sea World. They develop their worldviews in Washington, DC. They discuss following Jesus while walking in His footsteps in Israel.

I recently had a conversation with SLU founder Dr. Jay Stacks about the famous Dream Session he gives to freshmen entering SLU. I asked him what surprised him about the way students of different cultures and backgrounds respond to the invitation to dream. He told me that when he invites high school students living anywhere outside of America to dream, he has to cut them off from writing after thirty minutes. But American students struggled even to find something to write. He has to remind students what a dream is and tell them not to look at someone else's paper. American students don't dream because they find it challenging to hope in anything beyond themselves.

We have a hard time dreaming because a "You are the center of the universe" message dominates our everyday experiences. We're being directly applauded (or "liked"—you know what I'm talking about!) for putting our hope in ourselves. We hesitate to dream because we're urged to be important: to be liked and followed based on our attractiveness. "I'm the center of the universe" is the polar opposite of "I have a dream." Because being the center of everything ends right there—with one person. One very lonely, trapped person. Dreams extend beyond us—dreams help us reach outside of ourselves.

It should come as no surprise that we, as a society, are raising anxious kids. Our culture is screaming at our kids to put their hope in themselves and what they have to offer. They are not-so-subtly told to post pictures of themselves doing important things, to incessantly tweet out their own opinions on controversial topics, and urged to—above all—"Believe in yourself!"

The problem, of course, is that placing your hope in yourself doesn't actually work. It's like trying to pull yourself up by your own bootstraps. Ever tried it? And so the result is anxiety. The young adults I have worked with have stopped dreaming and instead lie awake at night in anxiety. It's hard to dream when it feels impractical and unproductive to rest (which is required to dream).

Martin Luther King, Jr. dreamed. He had a secure biblical hope that one day God *will* return and things *will* change. Dr. King dreamed because he had hope outside himself. And we can too. Justice will roll like a river. Mercy will come. God will not fail. We *get* to play an active part in God's planned future by believing in it and working toward it today. It's not something we must do to prove we're worthy of hope; it's something we can do because our hope is secure. We are not earning our way *into* hope; we are living *out* of it.

Is your hope in God transforming your life today? Are you living with a hope that is secure, or are you content with the secular definition of hope? Are you consumed by anxiety, holding out and hoping things *might* get better one day? Or have you given up entirely and begun to find creative ways to make peace with despair?

God's Inheritance

There's another astounding truth to God's hope. Not only does it give us passion in the present, it changes our own view of ourselves.

Paul prayed in Ephesians 1 that God would give us wisdom and revelation to know Him better. He continues, praying for our hearts to be made aware of the hope to which He has called us, to see the riches of His glorious inheritance in His holy people (Ephesians 1:18). By "His holy people," Paul is referring to all Christians.

God has something so valuable to Him that He would refer to it as His inheritance (Ephesians 1:14).[4] And what is it? It's His holy people; it's you and me. Paul is praying for us to become aware of our value to God, that we are His most valued possession, His inheritance. God's been calling us His inheritance, the very best of all He owns, since He started revealing Himself to us. The Old Testament mentions over and over again that God's inheritance is Israel.[5] And because all believers (Gentiles) are grafted into covenant with Israel, we too are included as His inheritance (Romans 11:11-24). Don't move on until you consider this. Until you realize your value *to* Him, you're not going to live your best life *for* Him. You are valuable! Do not let anyone, including yourself, tell you otherwise.

As His most valued possession, God makes sure your hope and future are secure in His plans. And what is your hope for the future from God? Let's turn to His Word:

> Yet this I call to mind
>> and therefore I have **hope**:
>
> Because of the LORD's great love we are not consumed,
>> for his compassions never fail.
> They are new **every morning**;
>> great is your faithfulness. (Lamentations 3:21-23,
>>> emphasis added)

> Being confident of this, that he who began a good work in you will carry it on to **completion** until the day of Christ Jesus. (Philippians 1:6, emphasis added)

> Praise be to the God and Father of our Lord Jesus Christ! In his great mercy he has given us **new birth** into a liv-

ing hope through the resurrection of Jesus Christ from the dead, and into an **inheritance** that can never perish, spoil or fade. This inheritance is kept in heaven for you. (1 Peter 1:3–4, emphasis added)

For our light and **momentary** troubles are achieving for us an **eternal glory** that far outweighs them all. So we fix our eyes not on what is seen, but on what is unseen, since what is seen is temporary, but what is unseen is eternal. (2 Corinthians 4:17–18, emphasis added)

He will wipe every tear from their eyes. There will be **no more death** or mourning or crying or pain, for the old order of things has passed away. (Revelation 21:4, emphasis added)

> Then will the eyes of the blind be opened,
>> and the ears of the deaf unstopped.
> Then will the lame leap like a deer,
>> and the mute tongue shout for joy.
> Waters will gush forth in the wilderness
>> and streams in the desert. (Isaiah 35:5–6)

Our hope and future are secure because, like Christ, we will rise when we die. But, as Christians, we're not *just* left with hope that we will rise with Christ in the future when we die. We have been transformed from death to life, here and now. The Bible says the risen Christ is the *firstborn* from the dead. We, who once were dead, have been made alive in Christ. And the same power that raised Jesus from the dead *is living* (present tense) in us (Romans 8:11). The power of the resurrection is now available to us through His Holy Spirit. We have been given a portion of our future in the present. God is in our future and is also with us here and now. Check out Ephesians 1:13–14: "When you believed, you were marked in him with a seal, the promised Holy Spirit, who is a deposit guaranteeing our inheritance until the redemption of those who are God's possession—to the praise of his glory."

God's Plans for Me

I speak around the country about all this future hope and present purpose we have. One of the most common questions I get after I speak is this: How did you become a speaker? I usually give the one-minute story, but since you're committing more than a few minutes by reading this book, I'll give you more.

I became a speaker because I went to jail. I sat in that important room with important people because I went to jail.

As I said before, my great weakness was people pleasing. My friends were all shoplifting, so I did too. I was more concerned with pleasing them than doing the right thing.

When I was caught, the court had to give me consequences for my wrongdoing. After people wrote letters to the court on my behalf, the court decided my consequence would be to speak publicly to all the local schools about decision making and friendships. That consequence led to my future. The one where I'm doing work that I love.

Want to know how I became a speaker? I learned about my greatest gifts from God through my greatest weakness. Turns out, Paul wasn't kidding when he said that God's power is made perfect in weakness. Turns out, Jeremiah was more than serious about our God having plans for our lives.

Friends, the reason I'm a speaker is because I got arrested. The reason I'm a speaker is because I got caught. I was caught putting my hope in myself and pleasing others. I was broken before God and given a new hope. And I was given a future greater than anything I could have ever imagined. My hope is now secure.

God has plans for our lives; they are not meant to harm us, although at times they can be rough. They're plans to give us a hope, a future. I sat in a jail cell but found real hope. God, indeed, knows the plans, plans to give us a hope and a future.

If you have given your life to the lordship of Jesus, you too have hope. Not only are you promised eternity with God when you die, Jesus promised that one day He will return and make all things new. And, as if that isn't enough, His story of redemption is hope for today because His story is currently being written through us. All those who confess Jesus as Lord and desire to be with Him on earth will not only receive *an inheritance*, we will get to be with Him forever because *we're His inheritance*.

So, friends, it's time. Our hope is real; our future is secure. Let's dream again!

PART 2

"Then you will call on me and come and pray to me and I will listen to you."

—Jeremiah 29:12

CHAPTER 5

WHO BEFORE WHAT

*"**Then** you will call on me and come and
pray to me and I will listen to you."*

• • • • •

*God has good plans not because of what
we've done but because of who He is.*

My mom would give up her life for me. I know this because she has proved it: she's chased robbers out of our backyard, jumped on the back of a runaway robber at a grocery store, and met me with a hug of undeserved grace and unconditional love when I walked out of a jail cell. I don't know what it is about her and robbers—strange circumstances have a way of repeating themselves. I'm sure you've noticed this in your own life. At any rate, she is tough and athletic and selfless. She is my mom.

She not only defends me, she winds up in the dregs of life with me—dregs like driving a U-Haul across the state, unexpectedly, at an unreasonable hour of the night. Long story there, I won't bore you with the details. You're welcome. It was one o'clock in the morning, and we still had an hour left to drive a U-Haul up a mountain.

I was desperately tired, but I knew it was my own fault we were driving so late. So I clung to the steering wheel, staring out the windshield, determined to accept my punishment. My mom could tell I was fading. And she didn't hold to the same idea that I needed to fulfill this debt on my own. She grabbed my hand and kindly commanded, "Megan, I'm your mother. Let me take care of you and drive the last leg." I could read the expression in her voice—she was about to get her way.

What a moment! What a mom!

I pulled over. We each opened our doors and walked around the U-Haul to switch seats, and she took the wheel. She even gave me her coat for a pillow. I folded it up between my head and the passenger door. My eyes closed gratefully as she put the truck in drive. I let myself relax, content to be saved by the woman who was, as always, there when I needed her. I was slowly . . . falling . . . asleep . . . until I wasn't.

Suddenly my head bounced to the left. I opened my eyes and looked around. Although we were still driving, my mom was asleep at the wheel, and we were drifting across that windy center line.

"Mom!"

Her eyes flew open and she stomped on the brakes. Our heads whipped forward as she assured me, "I wasn't asleep. I wasn't asleep. I was maybe asleep."

"Get out of the car!" I shouted.

She glanced over at me, shrugged with an embarrassed smile, and pulled the U-Haul off onto the shoulder. I put the parking brake in its appropriate place for two people sleeping in a car—in park!

Now, I'm not saying that my mom is not trustworthy. But I can tell you that she is absolutely not trustworthy at 1 a.m., if what you're trusting her to do is drive a U-Haul up the side of a mountain. She had the best of intentions, inspired by motherly love. Her attempt to drive the rest of the way was her answer to my wordless call for help. I was falling asleep at the wheel, too exhausted to make a good choice, so she stepped in. But, as is often the case with human solutions, she wasn't offering the help I needed. She loves me as best as she can. She would give her life for mine. But she is still not perfectly trustworthy. No one is, except God.

Is God *Really* Trustworthy?

After his famous declaration—"For I know the plans God has for you, plans to prosper you, not to harm you, plans to give you a hope and a future"—Jeremiah transitions into what's next for the Israelites: "Then . . ."

Let's stop there. *Wait a minute,* you might be thinking, *is she going to spend an entire chapter on "Then"?*

Nope, I'm going to spend this chapter on what you need to know *before* we get to "Then." Here's the truth: if God is not trustworthy, then His words won't mean much to us. None of Jeremiah's words can be comforting unless we know the One who is inviting us to actively trust Him. We won't move *for* Him unless we know and trust Him.

So let me ask you: Is God trustworthy? Answer that as honestly as you can. According to you—your experiences,

67

your knowledge, and your faith—is God absolutely worthy of your trust?

For those of you who answered "yes," great. Keep reading. I want to explore His trustworthiness with you, and maybe give you some more language, ideas, and illustrations to chew on and to talk about with others.

For those of you who answered "no," let me reassert another welcome. I want to make a case for His trustworthiness. No case would be complete without some dissension. I want you along for the ride.

Most of you, I bet, are going to be somewhere between "yes," and "no." Maybe you're quick to say you do trust God, but your actions don't back it up. Are you acting out of the belief in His trustworthiness?

Whatever camp you're in, keep sitting with that question. The place each of us are at looks different for different people—some of us want to grow in trust, some of us don't trust at all, and some of us aren't actively trusting the God who we claim to believe is trustworthy. Understanding more of God's attributes can help us—no matter where we are—move into the place God wants for us.

Let's take a look now at some of God's attributes. As you read and learn more about who God is, ask yourself, "Knowing this about God, can I trust Him? And if I can, how does that trust affect my choices and actions?"

God Is Omniscient

A few years ago, some friends from Bible study and I had the chance to delve deeper into the truth that God knows everything. After our customary snacks and small talk, we divided into two groups and studied Psalm 139. This particular psalm covers more ground than just God's knowledge of everything. David reflects on many of God's attributes as he writes, "You have searched me, LORD, and you know me. You know when I sit and when I rise; you perceive my thoughts from afar. You discern my going out and my lying down; you are familiar with all my ways. Before a word is on my tongue you, LORD, know it completely" (Psalm 139:1–4). God knows all of us, more deeply than any of us can imagine knowing anything. We drank this in as we read the psalm out loud to one another, reflecting on it as we went.

We came back together as a large group to compare insights, and I was floored by the differences. One group came back with warm fuzzies from being known, and pursued, and cared about. The other group felt . . . well, nothing of the sort.

"Well, shoot, He knows everything I've ever done. That's not good," someone from the latter group commented.

It's not that either group got it wrong—we needed the insights from each other to get the complete picture here. As we read the beginning of Psalm 139, we should feel exposed. God's intimate knowledge of us *should* cause some terror in our hearts. This is why the Psalmist says, "You hemmed me in" (Psalm 139:5). Anyone who's ever experienced claustrophobia knows that this is not a positive picture. But don't stop there—finish the psalm. By the end it moves to a place of trust, love, and gratitude for God's omniscience.

Whether God's knowledge of you comforts you or terrifies you, know this: In His omniscience, God will always love you. As J. I. Packer notes:

There is tremendous relief in knowing that his love to me is utterly realistic, based at every point on prior knowledge of the worst about me, so that no discovery now can disillusion him about me, in the way I am so often disillusioned about myself, and quench his determination to bless me.[1]

Dwell on that for a minute—you can't disillusion God. His omniscience means you're never going to surprise Him or overwhelm Him. He knows all of your secrets, and none of them will make Him falter in His love for you. Talk about trustworthy!

God Is Omnipresent

"Big" doesn't begin to describe God. We use adjectives like that to try to get our head around it, but God is so much bigger than "big." You can't get around Him or away from Him; His presence is our inescapable environment. No place or person is inaccessible. Including time. Not only is He beyond all of it, He dwells in it. God is omnipresent; He is always near.

I mean this quite literally—God is present everywhere in the spatial sense. When I say that God is everywhere spatially, don't think that I mean He fills space like dust motes fill empty air. Nope. The dust on the left side of the room is different dust than that on the right side of the room. Each of those molecules is distinct from each other. But all of God is everywhere. He is 100 percent all present at every point in space. He is fully present in your current city and fully present in mine.

Psalm 139 makes the case that God is everywhere spatially in two ways: existentially and intentionally. Stay with me, this is good. He is everywhere existentially. In other words, he is everywhere because He is everywhere. Were He not somewhere—if there were actually a place that was God-forsaken, as we sometimes say—that place would cease to be. If He withdrew His spirit and breath, all humanity would perish together and mankind would return to the dust.[2] But Psalm 139 also makes the point that God is not only already wherever the Psalmist goes but that God pursues him there. He is not just existentially everywhere; He is also *intentionally* everywhere we are. He is both like the air we breathe and like a hunter pursuing his prey.

Not only is God present to all of space, He is present in all time. Get ready, this is mind blowing. The way someone on top of a mountain looking down can see everything happening at once down below is the way God relates to time. He sees it all at once. If we think, "God can foresee the future," we're mistaken. He is not trapped in the present with us. All moments are "now" to God. He sees everything in all time happening at once. Is your mind spinning yet? Rather than trying to figure it out, hang out in that place of awe—the place where you decidedly don't know everything and you feel amazed. That's called mystery. It's good for us. It leads us to worship.

C. S. Lewis put it this way in *Mere Christianity*:

If you picture Time as a straight line along which we have to travel, then you must picture God as the whole page on which the line is drawn. We come to the parts of the line one by one: we have to leave A behind before we get to B, and cannot reach C until we leave B behind. God, from above or outside or all round, contains the whole line, and sees it all.[3]

The implications of God being outside of time are staggering. If God is beyond time, it means the cross is just as "present" to Him as is our sin. He is seeing Jesus on the cross as He is seeing us struggle in our daily lives. Wow!

God doesn't, therefore, just see who you are; He is at the place of the person you're becoming. Which is why He is not as disillusioned with us as we are with ourselves. No matter where you're going, God is already there. It makes sense for us to call out to God and find Him in the past and present and trust Him for the future, because He's present in all of it.

God Is Omnipotent

God is also all powerful. All of who He is can accomplish anything He wills as long as it is consistent with His character.

Jesus proclaimed His limitless power and then proved it through the lives of people. He said, "For mortals it is impossible, but for God all things are possible" (Matthew 19:26). With His power He has chosen to create, destroy, control the wind and the waves, resurrect the dead, transform the selfish, comfort the brokenhearted, heal the sick, and save a wretch like me. And, He can do it all again.

God can do whatever He wants with whomever He wants whenever He wants to do it. Keep your eyes open, He is looking to proclaim and prove His power through your life too!

Now let me take a second to address some of our "If God can do anything, why doesn't God just . . ." concerns. This is where things get hairy. You may ask, "*If* He could have done something about [insert your firsthand horrible experience], why didn't He?"

Listen—I feel for you. I really do. Let me step into that question for a minute by saying this: Just because God *can* do all things doesn't mean He *will* do all things. The reasons He chooses not to move are never as cut and dried as we want to make them. Sometimes, it seems He doesn't move because He sees more than just now. He has a broader picture. But it's also not as simple as that. God is not a cosmic chess master sacrificing pawns to get checkmate. It all comes back to the trust we're trying to grow. Trust depends on a person, not the outcome.

We know that God can move and we ask Him to move, but whether He moves or not, we trust Him. Trust is Shadrach, Meshach, and Abednego declaring to King Nebuchadnezzar, "Our God is able to deliver us from your hand, but even if he does not, we still will not bow" (Daniel 3:17–18 paraphrase). Mike Foster chose to replace fear-inducing questions beginning with "What if . . . ?" with Shadrach, Meschach, and Abednego's words "Even if." "What if?" questions can lead to fear and anxiety whereas "Even if" proclamations build faith. In Mike's words, "the words 'even if' invite you into a story that is filled with faith and overcoming. It is a life filled with strength and resilience. It drives courageous response in our daily lives."[4] Trust says "even if" in the face of fear. Even though "God can," we trust Him "even if" He doesn't.

Trust is Jesus in the garden of Gethsemane, praying, "If it is possible, let this cup pass from me, but not my will but yours be done" (Matthew 26:39 paraphrase). Real trust in God's omnipotence means standing firm, even though you may not get what you want.

So what should we do to come to grips with God's power?

As Proverbs 3:5 reminds us, "Trust in the Lord with all your heart and lean not on your own understanding." This is a risk we must take. He is reliable, but it still feels risky to pray a prayer of trust and let go. The truth is this: Risk is part of trust. This is true in human relationships, and it's true in our relationship with God too. When you take the risk to believe God is powerful and trustworthy, you have the potential to see God show up because you need Him to. I wonder if the reason we don't see God's power is because we play it too safe.

Go beyond what is within your capacity, and you'll find God there. God hangs out at places beyond your power, places which require His. He is in the deep waters. If all you ever do is splash around in the shallows, you'll never see the power of God. That, I'm convinced, is why so few people see God working in their lives. They genuinely don't need Him.

God Is Omnibenevolent

Not only does God know everything, is present everywhere, and is all-powerful, He is also fully good.

The best definition I've ever heard of the word *good* is whole and complete, lacking nothing (James 1:4). And the fact that God made us in His image means we have the potential to bring goodness, to bring wholeness and completeness to brokenness.

In light of that definition, let's look at some of the mistakes we make when we think of God as "good." I know I'm not the only one who has ever defined *good* as "safe." But when we start equating them, we're not talking about God anymore.

C. S. Lewis beautifully depicts this in *The Lion, the Witch, and the Wardrobe.* Four children, transported to another world, are told that the king of this other world is, of all things, a lion. A talking beaver explains it to the children this way:

> "Aslan is a lion—the Lion, the great Lion."
>
> "Ooh," said Susan. "I'd thought he was a man. Is he— quite safe? I shall feel rather nervous about meeting a lion." . . .
>
> "Safe?" said Mr. Beaver. . . ."Who said anything about safe? 'Course he isn't safe. But he's good. He's the King, I tell you."[5]

God's goodness doesn't mean everything will be risk-free, but it does mean He is working in everything for good.

The other mistake we make is defining "good" by the immediate outcome—the one we can see in our limited space-and-time perspective. Think of it this way: you choose your perspective the same way you choose a pair of glasses. What lens are you looking through? Do you ever let the circumstance become the lens by which you define God? We look through our circumstance and define God accordingly. That leads to questions like, "How could a good God allow [fill in the blank]?"

But when you allow God's goodness to become the lens instead, you begin asking different questions. You might begin to search for something new in the circumstances. You may ask, "How can I locate God's goodness amidst this chaos?" And, if you haven't discovered it yet, you might ask: "God, how might You be wanting me to reveal Your goodness amidst this chaos?" Or possibly even, "How might I, created in Your good image, bring goodness to this chaos?"

If your heart is broken by some form of suffering or injustice, how might God be calling you to bring His wholeness to broken places? How might He be calling you to bring good to bad? I'm not denying the presence of badness; I'm just excited to remind you that the One who is omni-present is also omni-good.

God Is Predictable

We can predict God will act according to His character. We may not predict quite what it will look like, but we can predict He will be Him and will act according to His nature. This aspect—His predictability—gives us even more reason to trust Him.

God's predictability becomes clear when we consider the human family's history of disobedience. How does God, our loving Father, respond to our mistakes? He is continually rerouting us to salvation and redemption. God works in His people regardless of their imperfections to bring about the redemption of the whole human family.

Adam and Eve disobeyed in the garden, but God promised a redeemer anyway (Genesis 3:15).

Abraham and Sarah disobeyed by attempting to come up with an heir another way, even though God had promised them a son. God gave them their son, Isaac, anyway (Genesis 16:2; Genesis 21:2).

Isaac's grandson, Joseph, was sold into slavery by his disobedient brothers. But Joseph's Egyptian captivity paved the way for his whole family to survive a famine, anyway (Genesis 37:28; Genesis 50:20).

The Israelites were led out of Egypt by Moses, and disobeyed in the desert, making, of all things, another god—when their God had just parted a sea for them! God preserved them anyway, giving them His law to live by. After forty years of exile, He took them into the Promised Land, anyway (Exodus 32:21–24; Joshua 3:17).

The Israelites continued to disobey, asking for human leadership not God's. Many of these kings were disobedient, including King David. Sure, he wrote most of the Psalms, but he also disobeyed grievously, killing one of his right-hand men and taking his wife for himself. God carried on the lineage of Jesus through his family anyway (1 Samuel 8:7; 2 Samuel 11:15, 12:24).

After centuries of disobedience, and more bad kings than good, Israel was led into exile. And God led them back, anyway—their city was rebuilt by faithful servants like Nehemiah (Nehemiah 2:18).

And one day, in this rebuilt city, a man born in Bethlehem to poor parents would declare Himself to be the awaited redeemer. Jesus became the once-and-for-all sacrifice who gives every man, woman, and child access to relationship with God for all time. He was the final sacrificial Lamb of God that would satisfy God's justice for all time, for all those who accept it. His death provided the way for our sins to be forgiven. His resurrection cleared the way for victory over death. His ascension into heaven enabled Him to send the Holy Spirit to abide in us. And His Spirit empowers the church to live out the message of salvation. We disobey, and God finds a way to bring us back to salvation. Over and over and over again. This is predictability at its finest.

While God may *seem* unpredictable, because beyond our limited understanding He acts in ways we don't fully understand, we must ultimately know He is predictable in acting in accordance with His character. And His character is good. We can trust God because He will always act in accordance with who He is. He is all knowing, all present, all powerful, and all good. You can trust him. "Then," call upon him.

CHAPTER 6

THE MAN WITHOUT
A HOME

"Then **you will call on me** *and come and pray to me and I will listen to you."*

• • • • •

When we call upon the Lord, He calls back.
He calls us to obedience, not results.

I was introduced to Norm, a retired truck driver, through an email in my inbox. I smiled as I read the sender's email was Norminator@some-email.com. Norminator . . . this was too good.

Norm emailed because he wanted to volunteer as a leader in my young adult ministry. He had two simple agendas with "the youth" (as he liked to call them): encourage these boys to become men, and make sure they know the gospel in their guts. He was invited on board immediately, and I am constantly amazed by his razor-sharp focus in ministry. That's what Norm goes for, every time: manhood and the gospel in their guts. Maybe he's not the typical youth leader, but I didn't want typical results. Norm fits that bill.

Along with many other Norm-isms come endless stories of Norm sharing the gospel with anyone and everyone. He makes sharing the gospel sound so easy. "And so I shared the gospel with 'em" is more common on Norm's tongue than "How are you?"

After Norm had volunteered for a few weeks, I invited him to share at one of our weekly gatherings. He began, "This one time I was eating dinner in Jack in the Box, a man without a home walked in."

I was struck by Norm's word choice. The man most of us would call a "homeless guy" was, to Norm, "a man without a home." Norm portrayed the man's sad reality and reminded us of the heartbreaking truth: this man did not have a home. Who would any of us be without a home?

Norm described this man as out-of-control, disheveled, and belligerent. This wayfarer began yelling at the other customers and causing a ruckus. Not sure how to respond to this man's chaotic demeanor, Norm quickly called on the Lord.

God responded to Norm's request by filling him with compassion for this man. And as the man continued to rant, Norm lamented quietly, "God, this is not your best for this man!"

Suddenly, the man immediately turned his fit of anger toward Norm, shrieking, *"What do you want from me?"*

Norm met him where he was, bringing on a little crazy himself. *"Let's take this outside!"* Norm yelled back. The two quite literally stepped outside. Not for a fight, but for Norm to obey God's promptings to share the gospel.

I will share the end of this story later, but for now, let me pause and make this observation. Sharing the gospel can be uncomfortable, as uncomfortable as confronting a shouting man at a Jack in the Box. In fact, most of the ways we're called by God to follow Him will be uncomfortable. I mean, I can't picture a comfortable way to carry a cross. And isn't that what Jesus, the One we're following, did? And didn't He ask us to do the same?[1]

Calling the King

When it comes to Jeremiah 29, we usually just stop with "God has a plan for me! Isn't that wonderful?" But we fail to realize we have a part to play in it.

Throughout the Bible, from Genesis to Revelation, God's people are not passive recipients of God's plans but are active participants with Him in the realization of them. God invites us, His people, to partner with Him in the good plans He has for us and, through us, for others. So, if God's part is to know the plan (and have the wisdom, strength, presence, and goodness to make the plan happen), what's our part? Well, according to the next verse, Jeremiah 29:12, God says it is to "call upon me and come and pray to me." Our three-step part begins with calling on Him.

First, we *call* upon Him. Imagine standing outside palace gates, requesting a conversation with a king. It gets crazier, though, because the next step of the invitation is to *come*, which means that not only does He invite us to request a conversation, He also grants the request. He invites us into His presence! And, of course, it gets even more unbelievable when we discover that not only can we come into His presence, but in His presence, we are allowed to *speak* (step three). Our voice matters to Him. We are not simply coming into the palace to be told what to do, to be given our orders. Prayer is a two-way conversation. We are coming in to talk with Him, to partner with Him, not as equals, of course, but as His children.

For now, let's focus on the "call" part of our response. You might be wondering, what's the difference between "calling" and "coming to God and praying"? Let's look at some Scripture for context.

The first recorded instance of someone calling on the name of the Lord is in Genesis 4:26: "At that time people began to call on the name of the LORD." Why were men calling on God? Well, what we know is they'd been thrown out of the Garden of Eden, and strife and betrayal had plagued them ever since. Maybe they needed the courage to keep going in the face of all the darkness. A few chapters later, Abram built an altar to the Lord, and he too "called on the name of the LORD" (Genesis 12:8). In both cases, the callers were seeking protection and guidance. In these first few pages of the Bible, we see that "calling on the Lord" means seeking help, protection, and guidance from God. It's pretty easy to put ourselves in that place, to imagine a time when we need protection and guidance.

But it goes deeper than our need—calling on God is calling on everything that is true of Him. It is saying, both to ourselves and to Him, that we believe He is who He says He is. When Moses asks God for His name, God replies, "I AM WHO I AM" (Exodus 3:14). To me this means something like, "My actions speak for themselves." The name of God reflects the integrity of His character.

Elsewhere, Scripture equates "calling upon the name of the Lord" with professing faith in Jesus. Peter and Paul declared that everyone who calls on the name of the Lord will be saved (Acts 2:21; Romans 10:13). But faith is not simply the words we pray; it's also the actions we take. Jesus says it like this, "Not everyone who says to me, 'Lord, Lord,' will enter the kingdom of heaven, but only the one who does the will of my Father who is in heaven" (Matthew 7:21; Luke 6:46). Calling on the name of the Lord is more than saying the words of a prayer; it's living a life that embodies that prayer.

A call to the Lord is the desperate expression of someone who cannot save themselves. It's a statement of faith declaring Christ Jesus is our true and only Savior. We call upon the Lord because calling upon ourselves would leave us hopeless. But that's not all. There is more.

The More: Complete Obedience

In Acts 25, Paul appeals to Caesar. The word *appeal* here is the same word that is elsewhere translated "call." Of course, Paul is not calling upon Caesar for salvation; he was calling on Caesar to judge his case. But the story helps us understand what it means to call upon the Lord. As James Bales puts it:

> Paul, in appealing to Caesar, was claiming the right of a Roman citizen to have his case judged by Caesar. He was asking that his case be transferred to Caesar's court and that Caesar hear and pass judgment on his case. In doing so, he indicated that he was resting his case on Caesar's judgment. In order for this to be done Paul had to submit to

whatever was necessary in order for his case to be brought before Caesar. He had to submit to the Roman soldiers who conveyed him to Rome. He had to submit to whatever formalities for procedure Caesar demanded of those who came before him. All of this was involved in his appeal to Caesar.[2]

Paul's call on Caesar involved submission and concrete action . . . it involved Paul's complete obedience. T. Pierce Brown said, "That, in a nutshell, is what 'calling on the Lord' involves—obedience. You turn your life over to the Lord in his appointed way."[3] When you call on God, you're not just recognizing God and asking for help or answers. You're submitting to the One you're speaking to, and therefore submitting your plans and your agenda to His.

God has plans for you—but first, you have to lay down yours. Even after we submit our entire lives to God, we will still struggle with the original temptation to act as our own god. We naturally put our trust in ourselves and our ability to get stuff done and figure stuff out. The invitation to call upon God reminds us not only that we don't have to trust ourselves to secure our futures but also that we can rely on God in the present. Did you hear that? Let go of the burden of running your own life. You don't have to. The invitation from God to call upon Him requires submission. But there's even more.

The Even More: All Day, Every Day

Calling upon God is a lifelong pursuit. It's not something you do once; it's something you learn to do continuously. This is good news. God Himself commands us to call upon Him in times of trouble (Psalm 50) and promises us He will answer the call with rescue. We call out to Him and submit to Him, knowing He is trustworthy, knowing that the one who "dwells in the shelter of the Most High will rest in the shadow of the Almighty" (Psalm 91:1). Again, listen to the words of the Lord: "'Because he loves me,' says the LORD, 'I will rescue him; I will protect him, for he acknowledges my name. He will call on me, and I will answer him; I will be with him in trouble, I will deliver him and honor him'" (Psalm 91:14–15). Reread those words from our Lord and take it in.

But what if you're not in deep, dark "call out to the Lord" trouble? Well, first, thank God for it. Then shift your perspective about what God wants from you. God wants our little plans too. He wants every interaction you have with your family; He wants the words you speak to your friends; He even wants the way you stand in lines with strangers. He's not after only big-picture submission. He also invites us to submit our plans for the everyday moments as well. We must learn to think of "calling on" not as a one-time prayer but a daily discipline.

On the other hand, those who refuse to call upon the Lord are also described in Scripture, along with the results of their disobedience: ". . . they never call on God. But there they are, overwhelmed with dread, where there was nothing to dread" (Psalm 53:4–5). This passage nails it for me. Have you ever felt that way, "overwhelmed with dread, where there was nothing to dread"? Maybe it was a result of not calling on the Lord.

But don't stop there. Even when we refuse to call upon the Lord, He is everlasting in His kindness to us. In Isaiah 65, God says, "I revealed myself to those who did not ask for me; I was found by those who did not seek me. To a nation that did not call on my name, I said, 'Here am I, here am I'" (Isaiah 65:1). In His radical love, God even shows grace to those who do *not* call on His name. That's what He did for each of us as well. Even when we were not seeking Him, He was seeking us. Even when we could not call on Him, He called out to us. I can't quite comprehend the "why" behind this acceptance from God except to thank God for undeserved grace. His ways are not our ways.

When the Lord declares in Jeremiah that He is the one with the plans, He immediately inserts our next step: then call upon Him. In other words, submit. In other words, give up control.

"It's Mine!"

Uh, oh. None of us like this one. Handing over the reins of control is hard, but it's essential. This desire for control is not original to us. When Adam and Eve sinned, they were issuing a declaration of independence. They were attempting to usurp God's throne, to take His place. And ever since that moment, each of us has made the same choice. Since the original sin, we have been born with this innate desire. You don't have to teach a kid to grab something and declare, "Mine!"

We don't grow out of it, either. We still have the same tendency to yell, "God, it's mine!"

"It is my health, and you should give it back, God. I am so sick and tired of being sick and tired."

"I'm in control of my body. Everything else seems out of control, so this body of mine, I'm gonna control it! It's my body to starve or overindulge."

"It's my sexuality, and I should express it any way I want. My sexual desires are normal and healthy!"

"I deserved the promotion more than he did. That job should be mine!"

"My spouse just doesn't understand that my way is the best way to do things. Lord, help my spouse to change!"

"God, this adult child of mine is making terrible life decisions. It's my fault. I blame myself. My children are mine."

"God, I gave years of my time, energy, and money to this church. I deserve to have a say in how it should or shouldn't change. It's not what it was. It's mine!"

But God compassionately whispers, "No!" to the four-year-old in all of us. "It's not yours to control. They're not yours. You are not even yours. Everything and everyone belongs to me."[4]

God invites us to come to Him honestly and even gives us space to lament when life doesn't go the way we hoped it would. But all of those examples were not from a "wrestling *with* God" posture—they were about wrestling control back *from* Him. Being brutally honest with God is, in itself, an act of relationship. It's an act of trust. But yelling "mine" is different than crying out "why." Try it—you'll notice the difference.

In Jeremiah 29:12, the Lord urges us to call upon Him. It's not just a suggestion; it's Him inviting us to play a role in His plans. Call upon Him. Surrender whatever or whomever you've been clenching tightly in your fists. Instead, hold your palms open, asking God to open you up to submit to His plans.

You're Fired

Have you been calling upon anything or anyone other than God for help? I attended a conference where a speaker talked about making sure God was the source of life. During his message he poignantly asked us, "Who else have you been calling on as the source of your life?" It was like getting hit in the head with a brick. I knew exactly who I had been calling upon as the source of my life, and it wasn't the Lord.

I walked out of the conference hall and immediately called my husband. "You're fired!" I cried out, instead of saying hello.

"What conference are you at?" he replied, totally confused.

"Oh wait, let me start again. You're fired from being the source of my life. I am so sorry for putting you there. Will you forgive me?"

Spouses make crummy gods. Not only do they get crushed by our savior-like expectations, but we also are crushed by our expectations to save them. C. S. Lewis made this very point when he said that idols break the hearts of their worshipers.[5] Is there anyone you need to fire from being the source of your life? A spouse? A boss and his expectations? Where are you trying to find life outside of the true Source? Have you been calling upon friends? Or how about yourself? How are you holding up under all that pressure?

You can be free. God is not calling you to call upon yourself to create good plans. He's inviting you to actively trust *His* plans by calling upon *Him*.

Vine and Branches

In John 15:5 Jesus says, "I am the vine; you are the branches. If you remain in me and I in you, you will bear much fruit; apart from me you can do nothing." Your job is not to plot and plan and worry. Your job is just to remain. Be a branch. Stay connected to Jesus. Experience His life flowing through you, growing you, producing fruit in and through you.

With His words "remain in me," Jesus is offering us an invitation, not an obligation. How do I know? Because He says "if" this, then that. If you remain, then you'll bear fruit. If you don't, then you'll wither.

Notice, He doesn't use the word *should*. Far too many of us think of our relationship with God as a duty, or obligation. We think "calling out to God" is work. No, friends, lean in on this one. The invitation to call upon God and, in doing so, to remain in Him, is an invitation into the good life. Are you only hearing "should" when it comes to your relationship with God? Let me tell you, it may not be God's voice.

These passages (Jeremiah 29:12; John 15:5) invite us into life, not into some kind of obligation. Jesus said this much earlier in John 10:10: "I have come that they may have life, and have it to the full." God is inviting us to a more fruitful life by remaining in Him. As we call upon Him and remain in Him, yes, we'll be surrendering our desires. But ultimately, He'll transform them to become better ones.

So how do we remain connected to Jesus, surrendering to Him, drawing upon Him? Jesus explicitly says in John 15:10, "If you keep my commands [obey them], you will remain in my love." This, of course, raises the question, what are His commands? You will find them throughout the Bible, but for starters, you might want to check out Exodus 20:1–17, Proverbs 3:5–6, Matthew 22:37–40, Romans 12:1–2, and 1 Thessalonians 4:3, 5:18. In short, when we remain in Jesus, we grow in knowledge of and obedience to His will and His commands.

Perfect Love

Moments after Jesus gives us the famous vine/branch metaphor, He lets us know an essential truth: "As the Father has loved me, so have I loved you. Now remain in my love" (John 15:9). He says He loves us. Don't miss this.

Have you ever wondered how much God the Father loves His Son, Jesus? The only word that comes to mind is "perfectly." Jesus says, "*As* the Father has loved me, so have I loved you." It's the same! The invitation is into a secure relationship of perfect love. It's the same type of love relationship God the Father has with His Son. The One you're being invited to call upon loves you more than anyone else ever has, ever will, or ever could.

What are we called to do in response? Remain with Him. How? Jesus says, "*If* you obey, you *will* remain." In other words, remaining is obedience. And obedience is love. God's love language is obedience. Why does the Lord call us to call out to Him and come and pray to Him? He wants to posture our hearts as we enter His presence. He invites us to surrender our will to be transformed into His likeness.

Jesus then commands us to love others with the same love He loved us with. He's not tasking you to just love; He's inviting you to receive and then overflow His love.

We are called to love in response to His love. Anything God asks *of* you is something He's already done *for* you. Why does He ask us to give up our life? Because He gave us His. Why does He ask us to offer our bodies as a living sacrifice? Because He offered His. Why love? Because He loved us first. Why surrender our will to the Father? Because in the Garden of

Gethsemane Jesus sweat blood and tears as He cried out, "Yet not my will but your will be done." Jesus modeled a perfect life of calling out to the Father. Branches (yes, you!), hear me out, there will be pruning in this life submitted to Jesus. The One we're following went to a cross. Our job is to follow His lead.

Remember, you're the branches. Our Father is inviting you to play your part and call out to Him to play His. Like Norm did that one day in Jack in the Box. Norm played his part and called upon the Lord. The rest he entrusted back to God.

But What Happened to the Man without a Home?

Let's go back to the outside of Jack in the Box . . .

Norm shouted at the man without a home, *"I have news!"*

"I don't care about your news," the man shouted back.

"Well, I do. And I need to tell you something. God loves you, man. And based on the way we've lived our lives, we deserve to be dead."

"Don't you think"—for the first time in their conversation, the man stopped yelling and made direct eye contact—"I don't already know that?"

Norm passionately and tearfully continued, "Well, I have good news. Jesus died for you, man, and He wants to have a relationship with you!"

Norm continued shouting good news of God's love. He screamed details of how God demonstrated His love on a cross. He outlined specifics of undeserved grace at the top of his lungs. He just had to tell this man without a home, "Jesus really loves *you*, man!"

Norm shared the gospel because when he called on God, God called on him. Norm invited the man without a home to call upon Jesus for salvation and to let go of trying to control his own life. "Put your faith in Jesus, man!" Norm urged.

"Well, I won't!" he said.

"I bet you won't, but you should!"

"Well, I won't!" And . . . the man walked away with no interest in Jesus.

And Norm moved onto the next story in his sermon.

Wait, what? Was that the end of Norm's story?

Well, yes and no. I can't tell you anything else that happened to the man without a home. But I do know this: Norm's story was not a story of failure. Calling upon the Lord requires submission and obedience; it does not require our definition of success. God calls us to obedience, not results.

Norm shared the story because the point of the story was not the end result (God's part), it was Norm's obedience. Norm didn't even feel rejected when the man walked away from his invitation to call upon the Lord, because it wasn't his love he was sharing. He called upon the Lord and received God's love and compassion in order to give it away. He didn't love with his own human love; he surrendered his will and right to control the outcome and loved the man with God's love.

Reader, lean into your relationship with God this week and pay attention to the moments when you feel uncomfortable. God may be inviting you to play a part which could affect yours or another person's future. It's essential you get it. Hope for ourselves and for others is not found in ourselves and our good planning. Hope for the future and trust in God's plans is found in the active and obedient surrendering of our will to

God's. We must open up our fists and the things and people we're holding in God's direction and ask for His promptings.

God is inviting us to call upon Him, to remain there consistently, and then to obey. God may or may not let us in on the eternal results, the hope and the future for someone else. But He is inviting us to play our part, not His. We get to call upon God, remain there, abide, listen, love people, share good news, be filled with compassion, and then, we get to entrust God with the transformation—the fruit in our own lives and in the lives of others. And not just for those in Jack in the Box but also for those in our neighborhoods, in nearby cubicles, and in our households. Play your part—and let God play His.

CHAPTER 7

LORD, TEACH US TO PRAY

*"Then you will call on me and come **and pray to me and I will listen to you.**"*

· · · · ·

The purpose of prayer is not to share your agenda but to align with His.

Last year God kindly and compassionately invited me into a deeper prayer life. I was speaking all over the country to people about Jesus, and prayer, and trust, and what-have-you . . . but I wasn't praying enough. Gently, God pointed me toward the ugly, ridiculous distraction that was keeping me from prayer, the thing that I was turning to instead of Him. Any guesses as to what that was?

Yup. It was my phone.

It shocked me to realize how often I thoughtlessly turned to my phone when I was alone. Is it a problem for you too?

When we think about changing our spiritual habits, we

often point to very spiritual-sounding things. But, in reality, often very simple things stand in the way of our spiritual growth. A cell phone, for instance. I'm convinced it is more difficult to be a follower of Jesus now than ever before, due in large part to the distractions of the smartphone.

We long for connection and settle for social networks. Checking Facebook, retweeting something, opening the email inbox (again)—all of these actions help us feel connected, but only for a moment. The only thing that will satisfy our longing for connection is intimacy with God, but tapping the Instagram app is easier.

We can be entertained whenever we want, and entertainment, though not inherently a bad thing, can be used as a coping mechanism. If entertainment is our coping mechanism, then God isn't. If we use our phone to help us stay afloat, then the phone takes the place of God in our lives. We are dependent on it rather than on Him.

God wanted me to change my habits and admit my tendency to settle for something less than my heart was created for. I knew that simply declaring, "I'm going to look at my phone less" wasn't going to work. So I put some concrete reminders in place, replacing my social media apps with Christian apps on my home screen. In the Instagram spot, you will now find the brown Bible app. My email was replaced by an app for listening to sermons. My text message app was replaced by a Bible memorization app. Maybe this sounds ridiculous, but when I picked up my phone, I needed to be reminded, over and over again, of what I actually needed—intimacy with God.

We complain that we don't have enough time to pray properly, but as John Piper tweeted (believe me, I see the irony):

"One of the greatest uses of Twitter and Facebook will be to prove at the Last Day that prayerlessness was not from lack of time."[1] Ouch. If you think you don't have time to pray, I'd recommend getting a realistic sense of how much time you're spending on your phone. The simple act of moving around the apps on my phone was my first step, my little way of saying, "God, here I am. Can you teach me to pray?"

Why Pray?

God declares through Jeremiah, "Then you will call on me and come and **pray to me** and I will listen to you."

Why does God ask us to pray? Because prayer immediately shifts our focus. It gives us much-needed relief from self-absorption. Notice, each prayer begins by addressing God. As we look to Him we are simultaneously looking away from ourselves as the sole problem solver. Prayer also shifts control. The hardest (and best) part about praying is no longer being in control.

When I asked people about why they do or don't pray, a common response I heard was, "Why pray if God already knows everything?"

Yes, He does.

However, think of this. Imagine you just found out some terrible news about a friend of yours moments before you were going to see him. And imagine that he knew that you already knew. Would he need to tell you about the tragedy? No. But wouldn't you want him to? Wouldn't you want to hear it from him? Wouldn't you want to be beside him in his hurt?

If this friend walked up to you with full knowledge that

you knew they just went through a difficulty but then acted like nothing happened, you would question the relationship, wouldn't you? You would feel much less close to him if he didn't trust you, by talking with you about how he felt about the news.

Even though we claim to want a close relationship with God and believe prayer is important, it wouldn't be difficult at all to find a Christian who struggled with prayer. It would probably be a lot harder to find one who *didn't* struggle with prayer. That's not because prayer is complicated. In fact, just the opposite. Prayer, done right, is extremely simple, and therein lies our problem. We tend to overcomplicate it, to make it into something it was never intended to be. We make it obligatory when it's meant to be an act of relational intimacy. Prayer is the key to not only everything you do *for* Christ but also is your relationship *with Him.* All throughout Scripture, God invites His people to pray about everything and at all times. And I mean *everything.* You don't need to edit yourself in your prayers. Even our harshest, most honest words matter to God because in praying them, we're actively trusting God with the unedited version of our lives.

God already knows. But when we tell Him everything we are going through, even though He already knows everything, we are entrusting Him with it. Prayer is an act of trusting God. Even if you're having a hard time trusting God, admitting *to* God is the first step of trusting Him with your lack of trust. This is why the 150 chapters of authentic, seemingly unedited prayers in Psalms are so profound.

According to Walter Brueggemann, some of the Psalms are an embarrassment to conventional faith.[2] In conventional faith, we think of prayer as coming to God with a formula or when the circumstances are right or when we're feeling a certain way. But the Psalms show us we can pray about anything, in any amount, no matter what we're feeling. The prayers in the Psalms are real and gritty and all-encompassing. In the Psalms, we learn we can and should pray not only in adoration, confession, thanksgiving, and supplication, but also anxiety, depression, fear, doubts, anger, and even (dare I suggest) bad theology. In fact, of the 150 Psalms, over half of them are "negative" in tone, and yet they're in the Bible (for example, Psalms 58 and 137)! Dr. John Coe adds that in Psalms, you'll hear things theologically untrue but felt in the heart.[3] They are the cry of a believer who must stay in contact with God even in the darkness. The Psalmist doesn't hold back—God suffers quite a few accusations at his hands.

Here's the thing, friends, God can take it. I mean, He already knows how much you do or don't pray—and He still wants relationship with you. The first step is honesty. Your prayer could go something like this: "God, I don't even know how to pray."

Are You Okay with Being Needy?

As a college professor I loved keeping my students on their toes. One morning, I kept them on their toes literally. I removed the desks from the classroom and redecorated. When the students walked in, they saw a long piece of duct tape dividing the classroom and the TRUE and FALSE signs I'd taped to opposite walls.

At the beginning of class, I had the students line up on

the duct tape. I could see the expressions on their faces—here she goes again!

"I'm going to read a list of statements," I began. "With each statement, you need to decide if it is true or false in your life. Then walk toward the corresponding sign. Easy enough, right?"

They looked around at each other, shrugging and smiling.

To warm up the crowd, I began with some real softballs. "True or false, cheerleading is a sport!" The class started moving across the room.

"It's impossible to touch your elbow with your tongue." That one was at least entertaining.

As the activity continued, the statements got harder to respond to honestly:

"I am not as confident as you would think."

"I rarely admit that I don't understand."

"I pray a good amount."

"I have things under control."

"I am needy."

I had designed this exercise to teach the students it's okay to have needs. Each time I did this exercise, I looked forward to the class's response to the "I am needy" statement. I can only imagine what went through people's minds. Some of them glanced to the "false" side right away, but it took a minute for everyone to move.

"I mean, I need God." I could almost hear their thoughts. "But I'm not a needy person. I don't want to be thought of as needy."

"I think I have things pretty managed, but I need basic things like food and air but . . . I wonder what she means by needy."

"Compared to others, though, I don't need much."

Let me ask you, how okay are you with being needy? Now I realize that "needy" comes across as derogatory. Let me reword it. Would you agree that we all have needs?

In our culture, humility and dependence are not virtues. We value independence and self-sufficiency, but this is not the culture of the kingdom. Jesus says the greatest in the kingdom is the one who approaches it like a child, that is, needy, lowly. In fact, He says we won't even get in unless we take the lowly position of a child (Matthew 18:1–4).

But we refuse to be dependent. We will only pray if we need Him. We don't pray often because we're convinced we can get by on our own, so we do. This is why we experience such increased passion in our prayer lives when things go sideways. When life goes wrong, we get desperate, and our desperation drives us to our knees. But when things are going well, we assume we're in control and have no need of help. The challenge, then, is to actively cultivate a humble desperation even when things are good. A commitment to a rich, authentic prayer life begins with your need.

Did you know that it's okay to not have the answers? Seems obvious, but we don't act like it. Here's the truth: Being okay with your own level of not-knowing is a good life posture. If we don't assume this posture, we can never learn anything. All meaningful growth begins with humility. If you can admit you don't know everything, you're more eager to learn something. When you're more eager to learn something, you release the burden of coming across as knowledgeable and, rather, become interested in others and what they know. If you think of yourself as "interested" instead of "interesting," you'll encourage others, grow in knowledge, and find God more often. And isn't that what the posture of a disciple should be? Humble and interested?

How Is Not the Issue. *Who* Is.

Look to the example of the disciples in the book of Luke. Jesus's closest buddies make a humble request, "Lord, teach us to pray," and, in doing so, admitted that they struggled with prayer. They recognized a fundamental difference between the way they prayed and the way Jesus prayed. So they did something smart. They talked to Jesus about it.

Nowhere else in the Gospel narratives (the books of Matthew, Mark, Luke, and John) are the disciples recorded asking Jesus *how to* do anything, yet in the book of Acts, the apostles end up doing a lot of the same things Jesus did: they performed miraculous healings (Acts 3:7–11; 9:32–35; 14:8–18), prison doors were miraculously opened more than once (Acts 5:19; 12:10; 16:26), and Peter even raised someone from the dead (Acts 9:39–42). The apostles never asked how to heal or perform miracles, but they did have questions about prayer. Relationship (prayer) comes first—it's the priority—and all of the work flows out of it.

The order is important here. Specifically, the disciples didn't ask "how" to pray, they hoped Jesus would teach them "to pray." Not so much about a technique but about a heart. If prayer is about relationship, then "how" is not the issue. "Who" is the issue. Which, of course, is why Jesus starts His lesson in prayer with a vision of the One to whom they're praying. I wonder if that's our struggle too. Maybe it's not that we don't know how, but we don't understand why. Or, perhaps more often, we don't understand Who. So we don't.

But there's something important to notice about the disciples' request. They didn't come asking to get but to learn. They didn't approach with a list of things they wanted God to hear from them. They came instead wanting to hear from God. They came humbly into the presence of One far greater, and the request was answered.

The disciples' request for prayer training is a demonstration of this needy posture. Humility is the gateway to a meaningful relationship with Him. When you're needy and hungry, you'll find freedom through dependence and also be fed. You will even learn a thing or two. So let's do a posture check. Are you willing to admit that you need help? Have you ever told God that you don't know how to pray?

Jesus Prayed

So what did the disciples learn from Jesus about prayer? Let's take a look.

Luke first records Jesus praying in Luke 3:21. Luke doesn't record the exact words of Jesus's prayer. Rather, he focuses on the incredible, immediate response Jesus received. Heaven was opened and the Holy Spirit descended on Him in bodily form like a dove and a voice from heaven spoke: "You are my Son, whom I love; with you I am well pleased" (Luke 3:22). Jesus received His identity and was reminded of His worth and position *as* He was praying. Wow! Is it any wonder that the disciples wanted to learn how to pray like Jesus if that's the kind of stuff that happened when He prayed?

After His baptism, Jesus's public ministry began. He preached and taught and healed, and soon crowds began to follow Him everywhere. But in spite of public demand and popularity, Jesus maintained His rhythms of prayer and dependence on His Father. Jesus said "no" to all sorts of things, all sorts of good things, all sorts of ministry things, so that He could say "yes" to His Father. As Luke reports, "The news about [Jesus] spread all the more, so that crowds of people came to hear him and to be healed of their sicknesses. But Jesus often withdrew to lonely places and prayed" (Luke 5:15–16).

Jesus *often* got away to lonely places and prayed. For Jesus, pleasing God trumped people pleasing. Intimacy with God was Jesus's priority.

We must prioritize intimacy with God because no one else is going to prioritize it for us. This world will often do just the opposite; it will distract us with all sorts of "urgent" and "important" things, while we forget about the most important thing of all. Are you exhausted because of the work you've been doing for God? Jesus didn't lead you there. Jesus was never too tired to pray—He was too tired to *not* pray.

The Perfect Prayer

After watching Jesus's habits and rhythms, it's no wonder Jesus's disciples asked Him for some prayer training. And Jesus responds with the perfect prayer:

"When you pray, say:

> "'Father,
> hallowed be your name,
> your kingdom come.
> Give us each day our daily bread.
> Forgive us our sins,
>   for we also forgive everyone who sins against us.
> And lead us not into temptation.'" (Luke 11:2–4)

The Lord's Prayer makes three petitions about God followed by three about us. Here's the first point I want to make: We're not meant to rush into prayer and give our shopping list of needs. The purpose of prayer is not to share *our* agenda with God but to align ourselves with *His* agenda for *us*. So we start by remembering who He is.

Jesus starts the prayer with a reminder of the relationship when He invites us to pray to Abba, our "Father." The word *Abba* in Aramaic is correctly translated "father," but it's a common and intimate word. For us, the word *Father* is often formal, but *abba* is one of the first words a child would learn. It's tender and affectionate. You can hear the simple syllables and imagine a baby mouthing the words. That's the depth of intimacy and relationship here.

Jesus could have given us innumerable other titles to address God with: King maybe. Or how about Lord? Nope! Jesus chose Father! Why? Because if we address God as king, our approach would be that of a servant, and prayer would become our duty. In inviting us to address Him as our Father, Jesus invites us to approach God as His beloved child.

Let me ask you this, do you pray to encounter God as His

child or as His duty-bound servant? Do the words *personal* and *intimate* define your prayers? When you think of prayer, if you're hearing in your soul: "You *should* pray more," you are thinking like a servant. The true measure of your spiritual disciplines is how you feel when you don't do them. Do you feel guilty or do you feel thirsty?[24] If you feel guilty every time you don't wake up early to pray, you're missing the point. God is your Father, not your taskmaster.

The prayer continues, "Hallowed be thy name. Thy kingdom come."

After we remember we are God's beloved children, we remember He's hallowed. He's set apart. He's holy. Remembering His character is the way we praise God.

We also remind ourselves that the kingdom is His. We like to think of kingdoms as ours. We think our life should be like the Magic Kingdom, the happiest place on earth. But when we pray we should not seek our own happiness and comfort, but rather God's kingdom and glory to come. Which, as it turns out, is actually the place we will find the greatest joy and satisfaction.

Here's the mindset you need before you move on to your requests: God is our Father, He is holy, and we long for His kingdom to come.

Prayer is not about us, but it involves us. God believes our needs are significant, which is why He included them in this prayer. Jesus continues, "Give us each day our daily bread, forgive us our sins for we also forgive everyone who sins against us. And lead us not into temptation but deliver us from evil."

So, yes, God cares about our needs, but notice what Jesus does here. First, He makes our needs subordinate to the will of God. It's His kingdom that comes first, not ours. And then, when His kingdom is the priority, our needs change. The things we thought were most important fade while things like "daily bread," "forgiveness," and "guidance" grow in importance. Notice, also, Jesus doesn't teach us to pray for our circumstances to change. He's not the only one. In all of Paul's prayers recorded in Scripture there are no appeals for God to change any part of their circumstances.[5]

Who could know us and our needs better than Jesus? That's what's so perfect about prayer. When we come with a posture of neediness, our needs can be met. We need daily bread. Bread represents our daily needs. We pray for daily bread because we need God to provide oxygen, clean water, and food. We need shelter, sleep, and clothing. Thanks be to God for remembering to provide for the needs we fail to acknowledge.

Even more supreme than tangible needs, we need safety, places to be fully ourselves, and people to do life with. We need intimacy with God, eternal salvation, purpose, hope, and everlasting love.

Like the Israelites who received just enough bread from God each day in the wilderness, we ask God to provide our daily needs as well. In prayer, Jesus invites us to ask for provision for today because tomorrow has enough worry of its own.

We also need to forgive. It's weird to hear forgiveness phrased as a need, because we often don't think of it that way. But here's the truth: not only do we need forgiveness for ourselves, but we also need to forgive others. Like Mike Foster says, "Forgive them. All of your thems. The more thems you can forgive, the lighter you'll feel."[6]

Lastly, we need to be led away from temptation. Christian leaders are followers first. "Follow me" were the first words Jesus's disciples heard and the last words spoken to Peter (Matthew 4:19; John 21:22). Jesus did not recruit leaders for His ministry. He was looking for followers. So come to Him and pray to Him—and come thirsty and needy. Prayer is not what your heavenly Father wants *from* you; it's something our perfect heavenly Father wants *for* you.

God Listens

Not only does the Lord invite us to pray to Him, He gives us an immediate reason in Jeremiah 29:12 as to why. He listens to us. "Then you will call on me and come and pray to me, **and I will listen to you.**"

Max Lucado writes about the moment Mary and Martha told Jesus about the sickness of their brother Lazarus. In John 11, the sisters said, "Lord, the one you love is sick." The sisters don't base their appeal on the imperfect love of the one in need, but on the perfect love of God. They don't say, "The one *who loves you* is sick." Instead, they say, "The one *you love* is sick." Lucado wrote, "The power of the prayer, in other words, does not depend on the one who makes the prayer, but on the one who hears the prayer. We can and must repeat the phrase in manifold ways, 'The one you love is tired, sad, hungry, lonely, fearful, depressed.'"[7]

While the words of our prayers will vary, God's response does not change. God listens. In Lucado's words, "He silences heaven, so he won't miss a word. He hears the prayer."[8] Which, of course, is what Jesus prays when He's standing in front of

Lazarus's tomb: "Father, I thank you that you have heard me. I knew that you always hear me, but I said this for the benefit of the people standing here, that they may believe that you sent me" (John 11:41–42).

Now that we know that we're heard from our first halting hello, let's talk about how to say "good-bye." What's the best way to end a prayer? Well, we pray "in Jesus's name." Let me clarify this is not just a magical sign-off guaranteeing the success of our prayers. If we are praying to God as "Father," we don't have to end with the words "in Jesus's name." This is because we cannot approach God as our Father unless Jesus, His Son, did everything for us. To begin with "Father" is to say, "God, I don't deserve this relationship with You. I only have this relationship with You to come as Your child because Your one and only Son took my place and offers us His place, as God's children." We end "In Jesus's name" to be reminded how it's possible that we can pray and have a relationship with God in the first place.

The moment you believe in Christ Jesus and His atonement for your sins, you move from being an outcast, an enemy of God, to a dearly loved child. You believe in Him, and God treats you as if you deserve what Jesus deserved on your behalf. Always remember, there is one significant prayer from Jesus that God seemingly did not answer—Jesus's prayer to be delivered from the cross. That changed everything for us. As Timothy Keller wrote, "We know God will answer us when we call because one terrible day He did not answer Jesus when He called. . . . Jesus's prayers were given the rejection that we sinners merit so that our prayers could have the reception that He merits."[9]

Jesus deserved intimacy with the Father; we deserved to be distant. Jesus experienced distance from God on the cross so that we would never have to be separated from God. He paid the penalty, and in His resurrection proved His power to make dead things alive. To pray "Father" is to pray humbly, admitting your need for Jesus, admitting your need for His sacrifice and the very thing Jesus needed: to submit and obey to the Father, for His glory.

Lord, teach us to pray!

PART 3

"You will seek me and find me when you seek me with all your heart."

—Jeremiah 29:13

CHAPTER 8

AMAZING BYPRODUCT, TERRIBLE GOAL

*"**You will seek me** and find me when you seek me with all your heart."*

• • • • •

Seek God over His benefits. You'll find what you're looking for.

The format of our book study was simple: read the Gospel of Mark and ask questions about the life of Jesus alongside people with varying beliefs about Him. My husband and I knew it would be a challenge for our Christian friends. We were asking them to just show up—to pocket their interesting facts, favorite sermon points, and clever quotes and simply learn about Jesus from the text. The study had one central aim: seek and find Jesus.

We invited ten churchgoing friends to come and bring a

few of their friends who didn't follow Jesus. By the way, people from all kinds of religious backgrounds are surprisingly receptive to studying the life of Jesus two thousand years after He walked the earth. He's a regular on the cover of *Time* magazine, His teachings are quoted as common wisdom, and some of the most influential (non-Christian) thinkers have been absolutely enthralled by Jesus (Gandhi and Einstein, among others).[1] Talking about Jesus tends to intimidate Christians more than their non-believing friends. Case in point: we invited my childhood friend, Colin.

Let me give you some context. People love being around Colin. Was it because he would line his truck bed with a plastic tarp, fill it up with water, and initiate conversations with neighbors from his driveway in his makeshift hot tub? Possibly. He came to my sister's wedding dressed as a sailor, got drunk, and swore his way around the reception. He was the true idiom of "the life of the party."

Colin had never been invited to a book study before, and he was intrigued. After his initial interest I told him the book we would be studying would be . . . the Bible.

"The ole bait and switch, eh?" he asked.

"Call it what you want. I'm not going to push my beliefs on you."

"I've heard that one before."

"I'm serious! I want to read it totally open to whatever the Bible has to say about Jesus. I want to see Him from a new perspective. In that respect, I have much to learn from you. If this is going to work, we need some different perspectives . . . perspectives like yours."

"Maybe I'll come."

On the night of the study, our living room filled up with twenty-four people. To my surprise, one of them was Colin. Together, we opened up the Good Book. As we started reading and making initial comments I noticed a huge problem: my Christian friends had only brought more Christian friends. Everyone in the room already had a deep faith in Jesus. Everyone, except Colin.

Have you ever listened to a sermon next to someone who you know doesn't believe in Jesus? You listen differently, don't you? That night, I worried about how uncomfortable Colin must have felt. He had likely never read that first chapter in the book of Mark; now he was reading it surrounded by unintentional know-it-alls. Everyone made great points. Everyone was connecting the dots. Everyone was impressing everyone. And then Colin chimed in . . .

"What the hell?"

This jarring but apt insight was Colin's sailor-mouth response to Jesus's baptism in chapter 1. Everyone drew up short. Jaws dropped. Someone's Bible fell on the floor. He continued, "So the clouds just open up, which doesn't make sense, and a dove comes down and, what? Sits on Jesus? And a voice comes from nowhere and this all just makes sense to you?"

Most of us looked down at our feet, but a few friends took a stab at the answer to Colin's question. We were hesitant and unsteady. No one was getting impressed anymore. A simple answer wouldn't suffice, and neither would a beautiful theological explanation. The night continued with questions no one but Colin had ever dared to ask . . . at least not out loud.

Everyone was challenged in their faith because Colin took the purpose of the group seriously. Colin's presence began knocking down walls. We spent the night grasping for answers, sitting in silence, and waiting for the next crazy, courageous, honest thing that Colin would say. We all spent the rest of the night as uncomfortable as Colin must have been at the beginning. Rather than impressing each other by sounding smart, we were brought back to the purpose of the group: to seek and find Jesus. And when we sought to find Him, no matter how halting our steps and stuttering our words, we were not disappointed.

Seek → God = Find → God!

"You will seek me and find me when you seek me with all your heart."

Verse 13 of Jeremiah 29 is one of the greatest evangelistic texts in the Old Testament. It defines an appropriate approach to God and also presents an astounding truth: God is findable. When you seek to find God, you'll find who you're looking for. What a beautiful promise: We must take God at His Word and not add to His equation. Seek → God = Find → God! The problem, of course, is that we tend to add stuff to it. And adding stuff to the equation is actually subtracting. We end up settling for less.[2]

Have you ever approached His Word seeking something more (or less) than God? If we approach the Bible on a scavenger hunt for a surefire solution to one of our many needs, chances are we'll be left disappointed in God because He didn't hand us the answer to our problem. In reality, though, we need to check our equation. If you make yourself coffee, settle in a comfortable spot, and open up God's Word seeking some inspiration for your day, don't be surprised if you leave your quiet time disappointed. Not that there's anything wrong with coffee and a favorite spot. It's just that "inspiration" is not promised.

Ever walked into church seeking truth and walked out critiquing the pastor's style or the worship team's set? You were disappointed, weren't you? That's because you were seeking high-level production value and entertainment. And if no one's told you before, let me be the first to tell you—that's not what church is for. The church doesn't have the same goal or the same resources as Disney. Entertainment is not promised.

Have you ever approached prayer with the nebulous aim of "feeling better"? Of finding peace? Listen: prayer is more than an anxiety-fix. It's possible to truly pray and still feel anxious. Were you expecting instant access to warm fuzzies? Say it with me . . . "Not promised!"

So, what is the promise we can count on? If you seek God, you'll find Him. When we trust God in the present, we can gain peace. We might gain understanding. We may be gifted with hope, love, courage, joy, and all the other amazing byproducts of active trust. Those things—peace, understanding, hope, love, courage, and joy—are great as byproducts but terrible as goals.[3] If we seek what we can get *from God*, we may be left dissatisfied. If we seek *God* and develop trust, the byproducts are wonderful. He is who He says He is and does what He promises to do.

God is both the path and the goal. He makes appearances everywhere: His Word, our church, our schedules, our relationships, and even our family dinner conversations. Seek Him. Go into all of those places, but go with a different posture—the posture of a halting, inexperienced, needy seeker. If you do, you'll find that this approach changes everything.

Seeking God in His Word

The next time you open your Bible, make seeking God your goal. The fact is, God is all over His Word and His Word is all about Him. He is the main character, remember? The problem is, we often miss Him because we approach the Bible (*if* we approach the Bible) reading ourselves as the main character. We are accustomed to reading stories egocentrically; we have been trained to see ourselves as the heroes of the story.[4] But the Bible is not an ordinary book. It requires a different lens. We can certainly learn a lot about ourselves from it but only if we get the order right. God, then us. As Rick Warren famously wrote in the first sentence of *The Purpose Driven Life*: "It's not about you."[5]

When we start with God as the main character, then we can put everyone else in the Bible (and ourselves) in the proper roles as supporting characters, characters who are looking to Him, falling away from Him, and reconciling with Him. Once we understand who God is, we can learn from these characters as they interact with Him. You may find in them something you can relate to—a struggle similar to the one you're going through, a character trait you aspire to emulate—and this is good and right as long as we remember what all of this points to. Remember, the great promise is that when you seek God in His Word, you will find God.

Seeking God in Our Church

Certain things in life seem obvious. You should be able to find books in a library, bulk food at Costco, and nails at Home Depot. The same logic, though, doesn't apply to God and church. If you show up to church, it's not promised you'll find God there. But we can seek God in church. It requires a posture check. I know it can be difficult. But maybe changing your attitude toward the whole thing will help you seek God there. What's your default question after a service: "Did you like it?" or "What did you think about the sermon?" The problem with these questions is that it's not our job to critique. Jesus hasn't given us a church so we can observe and criticize it but so we can participate in it. Maybe the sermon was clunky or exegetically poor or just generally boring, but it's still entirely possible that the message delivered by that imperfect human voice was God's word for you that day.

Believe God is involved, despite all of the church's failings, and change your question. After the service, rather than asking, "Did I like it?" ask instead, "What did God say today? What did I discover about the character of God?" And if you're up for a challenge in dependence ask, "How is the Holy Spirit leading me to respond to that truth?" Ask the same question to anyone who went to church with you that day. Together you might find that God did speak in surprisingly personal ways to each of you.

Seeking God in Our Schedules

One of my favorite questions to ask a new friend is "What do you do with your time?" because people's answers tend to reveal their values and priorities. Where we place our time *is* where we're investing our lives.

I had a few new friends come to dinner one night, and we went around the table answering that question. I was particularly looking forward to Faith's answer—she was my new intern. On her turn to share, she lived up to her name.

"Currently I'm taking nine units in college, getting to know God, volunteering at church, hanging out with friends . . ."

I didn't hear much past "taking nine units in college." I grew up in a very driven household and always took pride in productivity and being efficient with time. I finished my master's program in a year and a half, beat deadlines when I wrote curriculum, and even did more community service hours than necessary after that time that I, you know, went to jail. No matter the situation, I found time and made the absolute most of it. Had I chosen the wrong intern? I immediately questioned Faith's lack of drive. "Why are you only taking nine units?" I asked.

"I want to live really well now, not just in the future," she explained. "I want to have time to serve the church I love. I want coffee dates with friends without end times. I don't want to rush my time with my Lord. How can I seek God first if everything else, especially my future, is the priority in my plans?"[6]

She looked expectantly at the person sitting next to her, unaware that she had just blown my mind. I sat there in silent embarrassment, thinking about what she said. I had confused intentionality with a lack of drive. Faith leaned over to the next person at the table, and asked, "What about you? What do you do with your time?"

I was still stuck on the way Faith was spending hers!

What does your schedule look like? Is there any space for seeking God, or is every single hour crammed with "productive" enterprises? You can't seek God in the time you have left over—you need to seek Him first. In fact, one consistent theme throughout Scripture is that God gets the first and best.

And to seek God with your schedule, you may need to sacrifice your busy-schedule-badge-of-honor. That doesn't apply to everyone, of course, but this does: bring God into the things you're doing. For some, it doesn't mean doing less. He has you where He needs you. He just needs to be invited in.

In order to get away with Him, you may need to sacrifice productivity. Doing this actually increases our availability for kingdom fruitfulness. It may cost us some of the productivity we would define as important, but it grows in us a capacity for the kind of productivity that *God* defines as important.

I need more practice in this. I rarely miss scheduled meetings in my calendar, but I've had seasons where I completely miss time spent with my God. Seek God first in your calendar, friends. Then, enjoy the gift of who you'll find.

Seeking God in Our Relationships

When we seek God intentionally with our time, our perspective on others changes. Our relationships become opportunities to give others the gift of God and to seek Him in others. Next chapter, I'll talk about finding Him in others, but in the meantime, what or who are you seeking with your relationships? In the interactions you have with others, who is the priority?

Are you the top priority in your relationships? This is the way it works for most of us. We are constantly using others to build or reinforce our self-conceptions. Maybe you put a lot of stock in what other people could give you. Maybe you have "your circle" where you feel comfortable, where everyone laughs at your jokes and knows your story. That's not bad, but do you stay there at all costs? Do you ever go outside of your comfort zone to talk to someone who's a little outside of the normal bubble? Do you waver when someone from your "circle" does something that hurts you? Admitting that you're at the top of your own list takes vulnerability and perspective, but I want to challenge you if you find yourself there.

Maybe you prioritize other people's needs above your own. Sounds selfless, right? However, often what you're actually doing is trying to earn other people's affection so that you can feel better about yourself. But if you're not finding wholeness and completeness in God, who is love, then your love for others is often a weird attempt at control. And this leads to all kinds of codependent, unhealthy messes.

Relationships are only lived out rightly if God is at the top of the list. We should not be at the top of the list. Nor should other people. To seek God in other people, we must put Him first.

Seeking God in Our Family Dinner

I seek God in the everyday by creating rhythms and committing to them—like the rhythm of family dinner and the conversations we have around our table.

Most nights at dinner, we take turns answering these three questions: "What was the high of your day? What was the low of your day? How did you see God today?" I love to hear the answers to these three questions.

If you decide to implement our rhythm, pay attention to everyone's answers to all three. Listening helps you learn how to love your family. Each answer my four-year-old gives to "high of the day" reveals how he feels loved and seen. My husband's "low of the day" reveals his opportunities to grow in dependence upon the Lord and inspires me to come alongside him prayerfully. My favorite question, though, is the one we ask last: "How did you see God today?"

We added this question after years of asking and answering our highs and lows of the day because we wanted to seek and find God. This question kept me accountable—I knew that someone would ask me how I saw God at the end of the day, so I was on the lookout for Him. I knew the promise given in Scripture, but I had my doubts. Who was the promise for? Everyone? Christians? Adults? What about children? Before I had kids, I tested it out with my nieces and nephews. The first time we asked these questions to my eight-year-old niece, Georgia, my doubts were settled.

Her high was a compliment from her brother; her low was a negative comment from her friend.

"And how did you see God?" I prompted her.

"I saw God while I was swimming!" She smiled confidently.

I was a tad disappointed. Did I not explain it right? Then she continued . . .

"You see, I was swimming in the deep end which is kinda like faith. It requires trust to jump in. It's scary at first, trusting God can be scary, but my oh my, is it worth it. Some of the littler kids were playing in the shallow end thinking it's the best to hang out in shallow places because it's all they know. But once they develop faith, they'll learn that there's so much more to life in the deep end, but it will require trust to jump in."

What. In. The. World. Yes!

WHEN YOU SEEK GOD, (imagine me smiling confidently as I type) YOU'LL FIND HIM!

Where did you see God today? Answering the question can jumpstart your seeking. Asking those closest to you will give you new ways to see them and help them grow. And you'll see God in the ways that others are seeking Him too.

Cleaning before the Cleaners

We can seek God anywhere, in all of our interactions, at any time. Unfortunately, we can be just as flexible when it comes to making excuses. Why don't we seek God? Well, to illustrate some of those excuses, I'm going to introduce you to two people who undoubtedly seek God.

I have learned a lot from my in-laws. They're not the type of people who voice the things I *should* learn from them; they are patient enough to allow me to learn it from their example. They don't boast so I'll boast for them: they're on their fifth round of reading the entire Bible in a year. They didn't stop in Leviticus—they've gone through all of it . . . five times!

One afternoon, I came over to find them cleaning the house. I asked them who was coming over, and I was surprised at their answer—their cleaning service. The cleaners were coming over, so they were . . . pre-cleaning? But if my in-laws do it, there had to be some kind of cleverness to it. Why would you hire cleaners if your plan is to tidy up before they get there?

Well, maybe it's not as crazy as we think. My in-laws' housekeeping practice mirrors what we're tempted to do in our faith. One of our best, most tried and true excuses for not seeking God is this: we're not clean enough to believe the promise for ourselves that He'll be found. I've heard far too many people sitting in waiting patterns, waiting to come to Jesus or waiting to even show up to church because maybe it's been too long since they've been there. Let me get that straight—it's been too long since you've been at church, so you can't go to church ... what about next week, when it's been a week longer?

The Psalms point the way. They encourage us to go to God in any state, not to wait until we have it figured out. The biblical call is consistently to come as we are. Some people seem to think that a holy God can't look on or be in the presence of sin. If that were true, how could Jesus come to earth? Why did He spend most of His time around sinners? How could He save us if He couldn't come to us? In fact, the Bible makes the opposite point: He came to us while we were still lost in sin (Romans 5:8).

Jeremiah 29:13 directly states that when we seek Him with all our heart, we will find Him. There's nothing needed before the seeking. The good news of the gospel is Jesus + Nothing = Salvation.[7] If we try to add anything to this formula, we end up subtracting. We find all kinds of mathematically impossible equations like this in God's arithmetic: God + 5 loaves + 2 fish = over 5,000 people fed. 100% God + 100% Man = 100% Jesus. God the Father + God the Son + God the Holy Spirit = One God.

Here we find another, related equation: Seek God = Find God. It's that simple. It's not Do Good + Stop Sinning + Seek God = Find God. Nope. It's not after we tidy ourselves up a bit that we'll find Him. There is nothing required but the seeking. There's no to-do list attached before, during, or after this pursuit in order to receive the promise of Him. We don't have to wait and have our act together, we don't have to prove we're ready to make better life choices, and we don't have to figure out the trick to quit sinning forever. The equation is simple: Seek God = Find Him. We don't need to tidy up before He does the deep cleaning. That might be a clever idea when it comes to getting help cleaning our house, but your soul is a different matter.

Our job is not to seek our own cleaning; our responsibility is to seek the Cleaner. But we must be careful to make sure we seek Him for everything He is, not everything He might offer. Not for what we can get from Him or what we want Him to be. And that's confusing, because the byproducts of encounters with Him might look like a cleaner soul, but that's just the benefit. We might be able to—for a short time—keep up the appearance of a cleaner soul, and trick ourselves into thinking we're going deeper in our relationship with God. But cleanliness (like every other blessing and benefit I've mentioned) is an amazing byproduct but a terrible goal. If sinlessness becomes the goal, then we'll find ourselves critiquing God based on how clean our lives become. We can't clean ourselves up first and seek God second. Cleanliness is next to godliness, it's true, but it's not just next to Him somewhere—it's right behind Him in line. God must come first, always.

What Are You Seeking?

If you haven't found God lately, ask yourself what you've been seeking. Are you seeking Him in His Word, and expecting to find the gift of His reality, not just comfort or inspiration? Have you been coming to His church with a humble, seeking posture, searching for Him and His voice, not expecting award-winning entertainment? In your time—which is all His, by the way—are there hours devoted to Him, for Him to come to you in ways you can't explicitly control? Are you seeking Him in your relationships with others—which, at their best, are gifts from Him and for Him? Do the rhythms of your life anticipate finding Him in all things? Are you seeking by asking others where they see Him?

Our relationship with God is predicated on God's seeking of us, but He still calls us to seek Him. In Philippians, Paul says, "I press on toward the goal to win the prize for which God has called me heavenward in Christ Jesus" (Philippians 3:14). His part and our part. As Dallas Willard beautifully puts it: "Grace is opposed to earning, but it's not opposed to effort."

Seek Him and find Him, but there is truth in the converse too. This is one of the great paradoxes of our faith—our faith is initiated by God, but our choice still matters. So, if you've never done it, make the choice to believe the promise. God not only promises to be found in the present; we'll find and be with Him in the future. He is our reward for walking by faith. The reward is not our healing. The reward is not comfort or pleasure or entertainment. The reward is God Himself.[8] He is the prize. He is the treasure in the field. He is the kingdom. We can't miss this. If you have Him + nothing else, you have everything (and another wonderful equation).

I love how David says it in Psalm 27:4:

> One thing I ask from the LORD,
>   This only do I seek:
> That I may dwell in the house of the LORD
>   All the days of my life,
> To gaze on the beauty of the LORD
>   And to seek him in his temple.

If a genie popped out and offered David one wish, his wish would be to be with God forever.

Your work is to seek; His promised response is to be found. Seek God, over healing. Seek God, over His benefits. Seek God, you'll find Him. And when He is found by you, you'll have everything you need.

CHAPTER 9

HOW'S MY DRIVING?

*"You will seek me **and find me** when you seek me with all your heart."*

$\bullet\ \bullet\ \bullet\ \bullet\ \bullet$

When you look for God, you will find Him everywhere... even in everyone.

H i, my name is Jessica. Are you calling to give a compliment or a complaint?"[1]

"I'd like to compliment one of your drivers," my husband responded.

There was a long pause. "I'm sorry, I think I may have misheard you. Did you say you're calling to give a compliment?"

"Yes, you heard me correctly. I'd love to compliment one of your truck drivers. I've been driving behind him and noticed a 'How's My Driving?' sign on his truck along with this 1–800 number to call to give feedback, so I've spent the past few minutes mentally noting everything he was doing right."

She couldn't believe it. She immediately got a case of the giggles. After ten years on the job receiving eight hours a day of back-to-back complaints about her drivers, this call was the very first compliment she had ever received.

In her amusement she urged him, "Please go on . . ."

He continued. "He was doing a fantastic job staying in between the lines."

She burst into laughter. "Please tell me more, sir. What else did he do *right*?"

Randy managed to be creative while still remaining truthful. "Your driver maintained an adequate distance between his vehicle and the vehicle in front of him. Your driver also made multiple lane changes and used his turn indicator every . . . single . . . time." He was on a roll.

Screaming with laughter, she requested, "Please say that lane change one again!" She wanted to jot down each word so she could accurately share the story at the next lunch break with the other customer service employees.

Before my husband continued, we overheard her boasting to her coworkers in nearby cubicles. "Hey, everyone, you'll never guess what I have on the line . . . a compliment!" She must've put us on speaker because we could hear the enjoyment from the other coworkers as we continued. She thanked us, and we hung up laughing, eyes peeled for any other excellent truck drivers on the road.

Since that day, my husband and I have aimed to habitually find the good in others. Since witnessing my husband's pastime of complimenting truck drivers, I've begun to understand the power of seeking to find the good in others too. And what is the very best "good" we can find in someone? God's image, of course.

My husband didn't mention God by name, but he did choose to find His image. He chose to respond to people in a way that illuminates the image of God in them. He chose to see the good, he chose to see the right, he chose to see God's image. If you are on the lookout for things to complain about, you will absolutely find them. If you are looking for the downsides to yourself and your experiences, you will absolutely find them. But we can find God everywhere instead. We can find Him in the unlikeliest of places—we can even find Him in people who haven't found Him yet.

Christmas Calamity

A few days before Christmas one year, my sister's house was robbed. The only thing left under their disheveled tree was shreds of wrapping paper. It was an awful sight. She called me right away, and I rushed over. She told a few friends and neighbors via text. Her wonderful friends sent kind text after kind text, but the tears kept flowing. Then there was a knock at the door.

We opened it, and to our surprise, there stood a group of her non-Christian neighbors, each holding a wrapped present. The contents of those boxes paled in comparison to the beauty of the people holding them. When they heard the devastating news, these people took up their precious time to brave the holiday craziness at the stores. My sister's phone kept beeping, keeping tally of all the texts from Christian friends, and the doorbell kept ringing, alerting us to more neighbors delivering presents. I was not surprised by the amount of people reaching out. My sister is a very good friend to people.

When my brother-in-law got home from work, I quietly pulled him aside. I was amazed by all the kindness I had seen, but I needed an answer from him. The atheists were out-loving the Christ followers.

"Why is the non-Christian community stepping up more than the Christian community?" I asked.

He thought for a second and smiled. "We're all made in the image of God, whether we recognize it or not."

God is present everywhere in His creation. Everything and everyone that exists reflects something of His nature, His power, His creativity. Like every artist, He is in His work. This is called the doctrine of common grace. Common grace explains the goodness of the non-Christian community. God's grace rests on everything because He made it. Again, this does not ignore the fact that God's grace is often masked by the stain of sin, but again, sin has only masked it, not obliterated it. And, of course, this is especially true of people. Made in the image of God, the nature of God is visible in us. Yes, we've been damaged by sin, but His image is still present, which is why we can see Him and see good in everyone.

Made in God's Image

In Jeremiah 29:12, God urged His people to call upon Him, to surrender their agendas and actively respond to His. This is an act of trust. And what's His agenda? Well, here's a hint: He created us in His image and likeness, and then He gave us a job: "God blessed them and said to them, 'Be fruitful and increase in number; fill the earth and subdue it'" (Genesis 1:28). Created in the image of God, Adam and Eve were then tasked with filling the earth. On one level this means they were supposed to make babies, but on a deeper level it was a call to fill the earth with His image and His character and to rule over and care for the earth in a way that reflects the goodness and love and beauty of God.

Spreading God's image throughout the earth has been the plan since the beginning, and we are graced with the same mission. In fact, Jesus's "Great Commission" is a restatement of this original mission: "Therefore go and make disciples of all nations, baptizing them in the name of the Father and of the Son and of the Holy Spirit, and teaching them to obey everything I have commanded you" (Matthew 28:19-20). Jesus came not simply to save us from our sins so that we can go to heaven when we die but, significantly, to *share* Him with others all over the world. He has given back to us the calling we forfeited to sin; He is enabling us to live purposefully, to fill the earth with His image by making disciples who love and obey Him.

Left to our own devices, the best we can muster is a dim likeness of God. But God hasn't left us to our own devices. He sent Jesus to show us what it looks like to fully receive God's character and to free us from tyranny to sin so we can do as He did. It is only in trusting Him—that is, seeking Him and finding Him—that we can accomplish the mission He's given us. We will fail, but by the grace of God and the power of the Holy Spirit, we will fail forward. There are as many chances to fill the earth with His image as there are moments in our days. As we walk with Him, He will empower us to increasingly reflect the character of the One in whose image we are made.

Find Him and Be Found "in Him"

With all of this talk about seeking and finding God, let's not forget the conversation we had about God's omnipresence. He is everywhere both because He created everything and because He is pursuing us. It's the latter idea that gives context to our conversation about seeking God. What does it mean to seek a God who is already pursuing us? It means that when we find Him, we will immediately realize *we're* the ones who have been found.

When we seek Jesus, we'll find Him and the opportunity to be found "in Him." God's plans are not based on us but on who He is and what He has done. They are not dependent on our initiative but on His. If it were left up to us, we could never find our way to Him. This is why He came to us, to show us the way to find Him. So many people misunderstand this. In fact, when asked about what it means to be a Christian, most people jump to some kind of action, like "love God," or "love people," or "do good works." Yes, we are called to do those things. But jumping to that answer is skipping over the most important part. The essence of Christianity is not *your* works for God, but *His* work for you. Your doing is a response to what He has already done.

Paul writes nearly all of his letters with a structure that conveys this truth. He starts with who we are on the basis of God's work and God's initiative—we are God's beloved children—and then shares what we are to do in response— love God and others.[2] One reason Paul uses this structure is so we don't mistakenly think that who we are *is* what we do. Our faithful work is a response to His finished work.

The six chapters of Paul's letter to the church in Ephesus, known as the book of Ephesians, is a perfect example of this. The book has two major movements. The first movement (comprised of those first three chapters) tells us what it means to be "in Christ." The second movement (the second half of the letter) tells us how to live like that's true.

In Ephesians 1–3, we find that we are "in Christ." Our identity is secure because of what He has done for us. The essence of Christianity is not what we do *for* Christ, it's what's been done *by* Him on our behalf. In order to make Christ known, we need to know that we're already found "in Him" before we do anything "for Him."

When you become a Christian, *wham!* You are now "in Christ." But you still have a lifetime of living into that reality. You are *already* whole, complete, and covered in the righteousness of God. However, you are also *not yet* who you already are. Theologians call this the sanctification gap, the gap between who we are "in Christ" and who we are on a daily basis. He has given us His Holy Spirit to enable us to close that gap in the *already* as we wait for and long for the *not yet*. Your habits and will change over time, even though the real change has already taken place.

Confused? It's like this. On December 11, 2010, I got married and became a wife. It was one and done; I was officially married. But I had twenty-six years of singleness and single-type-of-habits, despite my new status as "wife." There was a definite learning curve. Now, I spend my life acting more like a wife than a single person. I check in with my husband before I make commitments, we check in with each other before we buy stuff, and we have the "family in an airport" thing down.

On 12/11/10, I became a wife, but I've spent the past decade learning to act in accordance with that truth.

In the first chapter of Ephesians, Paul asserts that God's gracious plan of blessing can be enjoyed "in Christ alone." Paul repeats the terms "in him," "through him," "in Christ," or an equivalent eleven times in this chapter, emphasizing the importance of this distinction. Someone is "in Christ" if they've repented (turned away) from their life of sin and trusted Jesus for forgiveness from sins and for eternal life. And this "in Christ" identity is not simply something for the afterlife. Not only do we get life with God in heaven for eternity, we get to receive life in our everyday, earthly existence.

Once we see that we are "in Christ," then we can pay attention to the second half of the book of Ephesians and respond by *doing*. What are we to do? Be humble and gentle. Submit to one another. Obey our parents (Ephesians 4:2; 5:21; 6:1). These aren't merit badges; they are a response to God's extravagant love for us. We do because we are. I love my husband, not because my love will somehow make me his wife, but because I already *am* his wife. We love Christ because we're loved by Him. We do because we already are. This was modeled in the life of Jesus as well. The Father declared Him "beloved Son" before He had done anything in public ministry. Being overflows into doing.

Once we understand this, we are compelled to share Him by looking more like Him and calling out His image in others as well. You see, as we find ourselves "in Christ," as Jesus gives us a new identity and teaches us how to live out of it, how to fully be the image of God we were made to be, He also teaches us to do the same for others. It's not that we can save them or give them a new identity; He's already done that for them. Instead, He teaches us how to invite others into relationship with Him, to invite them to find their lives, their new name, "in Him," so that they too can be everything He created them to be.

The Power of Names

There's the name your parents put on your birth certificate, and then there are the names that you take on in life. For example, I've been labeled many names beyond my given name Megan. One of the consistent names was "crazy." I could hardly walk into a room without someone calling me "crazy." What can I say? I've got a zest for life! There were times I didn't want to be called crazy, so I tried to tone myself down, wanting to be named "normal."

I took part in naming others too. Some of these names were kind, others, not so much. Some people are named "fashionable," and others "brilliant." Some people hear themselves called "delightful" and "helpful." But the mean names go deeper and stick longer: names like "stupid," "lazy," and "ugly."

A name can break us down or build us up, show us who we're meant to be or blind us to it. God knew this. After He wrestled with Jacob ("he who strives"), God renamed him Israel ("he strives with God"). He renamed Abram ("exalted father") Abraham ("father of many nations"), pointing to his offspring Israel.

Names are powerful. This is why my family started naming each other at birthdays. Naming has become a powerful tradition in our family, a new way of loving each other by speaking truth and breaking open the potential in each other. My brother-in-law, who taught me this art of intentionally naming each other, has known me for over a decade, and I think he has seen the positive and negative effects of the name "Crazy." I'm often the one to get the dance party started at weddings, but I've found myself in trouble too. On one of my birthdays he thoughtfully renamed me "Passionate." I immediately felt the weight of "crazy" drop. He saw me as something more than a high-energy nuisance who needed to calm down. "Passionate" is crazy with a purpose.

Names have more power over us than we realize. What have you been named? Silly? Smart? Beautiful? Crazy? Creative? Outgoing? Introverted? How have they shaped you? What names have been given to you? What names have you given yourself? A name can either box us in or break open our potential. If we hear we are stylish, we'll run to the closet to find courage. If we hear we're a genius, we'll have a harder time admitting that we don't know something. If we hear who we are in Christ, we might run to Him when we need courage. And, in doing so, we might become more like Him. When we look like Him, we have the power to introduce others to God with our presence.

As you encourage your friends or celebrate birthdays, name them with true names. Let them know how you see God's image in them so when they seek to be like God, they seek Jesus. And remember the promise? They'll find Him.

Seeking Who People Are Becoming

What we seek in others is important because it dictates what we find. If we're not careful, we'll fall into the all-too-familiar-trap of merely finding and focusing on what people do wrong. If we *seek* perfection in our family or friends, we'll *find* all the ways they fall short. But there's another way. Rather than falling prey to human nature by seeking perfection, we can instead seek to find the person they're becoming.

What our community needs is not a perfect standard but people who seek to find Christ in others. If we want to see the people around us growing and becoming people who find the best in others, we need to seek and point out the best we find in them.

Luckily, we're not without a model ourselves. Jesus saw who people were becoming before they had arrived. From choosing unqualified disciples, to sharing meals with sinners, to the thief He forgave on the cross, Jesus found opportune moments to see who people were becoming. While we don't have Jesus's ability to see the future, we can take advantage of the present by seeking and finding the best in our friends and family. We can seek and point out the seemingly small, yet significant moments where they get things right. Not only does it impact them in that moment, it will impact their future as well.

I've made seeking to find God in others, especially my family, a conscious habit. And, my friends, let me tell you, we *have* to be intentional to do so. If we're not intentional, we'll drift toward a critical life—critiquing terrible drivers and complaining about frustrating people. I don't want my kids to live this way, and as their model, it starts with me. Seeking and finding God's image in my boys has become one of my greatest delights—and, as a result, they're getting to see more of God's image in me.

In seeking to find what others are doing right, we're modeling a lifestyle that is countercultural. How do I know? Because it took ten years for Jessica to receive a compliment on her drivers.

CHAPTER 10

FRED'S HEART

*"You will seek me and find me when you seek me with **all your heart**."*

• • • • •

Pay attention to what you're paying attention to. That which has your attention has your heart.

Before I was about twenty years old, I spent most of my Valentine's Day energy feeling annoyed. Not heartbroken or hopeful, just tired and annoyed. I was up at 5 a.m., on a reluctant mission to drop off anonymous cards decorated with outdated puffy paint to my dad's sisters. Every . . . single . . . year.

We drove for hours to drop off these anonymous gifts, which weren't even anonymous because my aunts knew they were from my dad. He had dropped off "anonymous" Valentine's Day gifts to them since back when they were in high school. We'd drive up to one of their houses, and my dad would turn around in the car toward my sister and me and make a shushing motion, and I'd just roll my eyes. I knew my aunts loved the tradition, but of course I would think it was *obnoxious* and *annoying*—I was in high school. But my dad didn't let my bad attitude stop him. He wanted his sisters to know that no matter what, someone found them special and worthy of love. Cute, I know. I just didn't think so at 5 a.m.

Now, I can't help but be thankful. At the time, it felt impossible to think outside myself, but my parents made it a practice to think outside of themselves, and they dragged me along if they had to. My parents claimed they were "thankful for family" each Thanksgiving over dinner, and then they proved it throughout the rest of the year. The biggest piece of evidence was where my parents spent their time.

"Time is money," so they say. I don't even know who "they" are, but if I met "them," I'd make sure to clarify. I'd agree that *time can be spent making money*, but then I would go on to argue that the most important thing about time is that it's beyond monetary value. You can buy a lot of things, but you can't buy time. Where we choose to spend our precious time is where we're choosing to invest our lives. And where we invest our lives reveals what's in our hearts.

All Our Heart

Jeremiah preaches the need to seek God with *all our heart*. What does he mean by heart? When Scripture refers to the heart, it's most often referring to the center of the human spirit, from which springs thoughts, emotions, and desires which lead us toward the courage necessary to act. Also wrapped up in the word *heart* is the notion of will. To do something with "all our heart" is to *choose* it. It is to apply ourselves to it with complete conviction and perseverance. "Heart" goes beyond what you know and beyond what you think you're supposed to want. Your "heart" is what you truly want and what you put your energy into pursuing. The clearest way to see what you truly want is to look at where you choose to spend your time. Which, believe it or not, is a choice. This is why I changed my token question for any new acquaintance from "What do you do?" to "What do you do *with your time*?"

Most of the time people answer what they do for a living, which is pretty normal. Stay-at-home parents greatly appreciate the slightly adjusted question and proudly share how they're currently spending their time investing in their kids. Sometimes, though, people ask for clarification. Of course, I love when they ask. It's a great chance to leap onto my soap box.

They ask, "Do you mean, what do I do for a living?"

I respond, "Not necessarily. I'm asking where you're choosing to invest your time. Where you choose to spend your time is where you're investing your life. If you merely answer with what you do for a living, I'll miss out on the reasons why you work there. Not only do I want to know where your time goes, I want to know *why* your time goes there. Oftentimes it's the reasons *why* we do what we do that showcases our priorities, those places and people most valuable to us. And the places or people you find valuable are the places and people who have your heart."

If we start the conversation with, "What do you do with

your time?" we blow right by surface answers and get right to the "heart" of the matter, like why we do what we do. Sometimes we even get into hobbies. Remember those?

My parents still invest their time being thankful for their friends and family. They throw annual block parties to love their neighbors, show up at odd hours of the night while friends undergo surgery, and drop off anonymous Valentine's Day cards. I'm thankful they live thankful lives, and I'm thankful for the practicum in how I should spend my time.

Speaking of which, where do you spend yours? Those people you say you value—does your time reflect that? The things you love to do—are you spending time doing them? If not, you might want to rethink your hours. If we look at where our time goes, we can discover where our heart resides. Your time is valuable. Choose wisely where you spend it. You're showcasing the location of your heart. And, of course, Jeremiah reminds us that the most meaningful place we can choose to spend our time, to invest our heart, is with God.

One of my favorite verses is Acts 4:13. A crowd considers the lives of Peter and John, notes their courage, and concludes that "these men had been with Jesus." Peter and John were uneducated and, at the time, practically unknown, but it was evident to everyone who saw them that they had chosen to spend their time, and thus invested their hearts, with Jesus. And that changed everything.

The Fate of Fred's Heart

My dad, Fred Fate, has done a bit of everything, and he's done everything with enthusiasm. Not long ago, my family started noticing a few things out of the norm. It started with a few missed turns on familiar drives, but eventually we took note of greater warning signs. We wondered if we needed to investigate more carefully. Finally my sister Kimi called his doctor and scheduled a checkup.

After some routine tests, my dad was informed, "You won't be going home today. You'll be having surgery in the next twenty-four hours." After a few more tests, our family and a team of doctors began planning the emergency triple bypass, open-heart surgery that would happen the following morning.

The morning came and our family gathered in the waiting room. Waiting is hard. And frustrating. Isn't it frustrating how often God calls us to wait on Him? But waiting is where faith becomes necessary, where our heart must get involved. Waiting is where God draws our hearts to their true desire. In waiting rooms all of our coping mechanisms are unmasked; all of the silly and meaningless places where we spend our time are stripped away. It all comes crashing to a halt, and God forces us to confront the real contents of our heart. He lovingly but surely exposes our wants as incomplete and unsatisfying, and then He pulls us close to Himself and shows us the true object of our desiring.

Instant gratification is the bane of our existence. The ability to get whatever we want whenever we want it is ruining this generation. It destroys anticipation, dependence, and joy. And it destroys faith. We wouldn't have to have faith in a God who immediately gave us anything we wanted. In the waiting and silence, our hearts do not just kick into gear, they're exposed. As long as everything is humming along just the way we like it, we never have to examine our hearts. But when everything comes grinding to a halt, we have no choice but to examine our priorities.

Waiting is invaluable. A few disciples waited at the foot of the cross and once again after Jesus ascended into heaven. They gave up their plans and their halfheartedness, and they waited on God. It was in the waiting room that I gave God the rest of my heart. I trusted His hand, His timing, and His plan for my dad. Because it's impossible to fully worry and worship at the same time, we chose to worship with all our heart as we waited. And here's how:

I asked my sister, "Remember how you scheduled a checkup for Dad?" We both smiled.

"Yes!" she said. "And remember when Dad didn't buy a new house a month ago even after he signed paperwork to sell his house?" We were all surprised that he backed out last minute.

She continued, "Whoa. The doctor even said he was one stressful event away from having a heart attack that would've taken his life because of the severity of the clogs in his arteries. Thank God he didn't move."

"Remember how we noticed the warning signs?"

We found God as we remembered. It was as if God had been waving His hands at my family the prior month, trying to get our attention.

In prayer, we thanked God for His presence, admitted our honest thoughts and feelings, and prayed for our desires. No matter the outcome, we knew God was with us and with my dad. We gave God all our hearts. We trusted God with our dad's heart with all our hearts in the waiting as we focused our attention on God's heart—to care for us.

God wants to get our attention through the details of our lives. If we're willing to pause and seek Him with all our heart, we'll see Him there. I'll never know all the reasons God chose to heal Fred's heart, but I must wonder if He also planned to heal mine.

God is trying to tell exciting stories of His presence through our lives all the time. We miss Him because we seek Him halfheartedly. We miss Him because we think He wouldn't want to be involved in something as ordinary as our lives. What a miss! God is always telling great stories, stories that will be found by us when we're fully invested in finding Him in them. Think over your past few days how God might be waving His hands to get your attention? What are you seeking today with *all your heart*? Are you seeking approval or achievement? Are you trying to be more productive and more put together? Have you given your heart away to other people's perceptions, or to your own image, or simply settled for a "normal life"? Pay attention to what you're paying attention to. Pay attention to who or what has your heart.

What Do I See—Problems or Promises?

When Jeremiah talked about God's plans to give His people a hope and a future, He was really talking about two futures at the same time. The first was return from exile, salvation for the people of Israel, but as we know, this future also pointed to something much broader, much grander, and much more enduring: salvation for all nations through Jesus Christ. All of God's plans for the future are made possible by and are realized in Jesus, which is why we can read Jeremiah 29:11 today, thousands of years later, and still claim the promise there. We are invited into this hope-filled future through Jesus. But this begs the question: how do we accept that invitation? How can we know if we're living into God's plans today? Simply by asking ourselves one question: "What have I been focusing on?"

We must pay attention to what we're paying attention to. Giving your attention to something comes at a cost; no wonder they call it *paying* attention. The object of our heart, which leads to our focus and investment of time, will dictate what we find. It's no wonder the words from Jeremiah 29 urge us to not just seek (focus) but seek (focus) with *all our heart*. As we discussed in the last two chapters, Jeremiah knew the promise on the other end of the seeking, that we'll find God. Consequently, we need to focus on that promise with all our heart; otherwise we'll default into focusing on problems. Like the ten spies in the book of Numbers. Remember them?

Here's a quick recap. The children of Israel were freed from slavery in Egypt, and God promised He would bring them to the Promised Land. God had delivered them out of slavery so He could lead them into something new. But the children of Israel were stumbling and falling prey to the temptation to stare backward. Their heads were turned in the wrong direction.

As a result of their lack of focus, the Israelites disobeyed and were sent into decades of wandering in the wilderness. Finally, forty years later, God opened the way for His people to enter the Promised Land. He told Moses to pick twelve spies to explore the land. These twelve spies spent forty days scoping out the land and came back with their report. Ten of the spies told the people that the land was just as God foretold. It was filled to bursting with milk and honey and every other good thing. However, the people were giants, the cities were fortified, and the enemy camps were full of fighters who could kill the Israelites quicker than they could sound a retreat (Numbers 13:27–29). With this list of complaints, they armed themselves with more reasons to long for what *was*. Since they focused on the problems, they didn't want to move into *what will be*. New can be scary. And this is where we must be careful.

You can't make mention of God's promises and then add your own "but there are problems." Of course there are problems! If you look for them, you will absolutely find them, and by focusing on them, you will absolutely magnify them. But the problems can't overshadow the promise. Where's your heart? It's right alongside whatever you are focusing on. It follows your focus, whether it's toward problems or toward Jesus. We need to fix our focus. We need to seek God and hold onto His promises with all our heart. We cannot just focus on God's promises, though; we must also focus on Jesus, who is the embodiment and fulfilment of God's promises. Yes, there are problems, troubles, but He has promised to be with us in the troubles. If we forget Jesus, the problems in our lives will look bigger than the promises, and eventually those problems will destroy us.

Instead of being like the ten spies who fixated on the problems, we need to be like the two faithful spies, Joshua and Caleb, who focused on God's promises. In fact, Caleb was so sure of God's promise that he stood up before the people, contradicted the other ten spies, and boldly declared, "We should go up and take possession of the land, for we can certainly do it" (Numbers 13:30) God rewarded Caleb's faith by declaring, "Because my servant Caleb has a different spirit and *follows me wholeheartedly*, I will bring him into the land he went to, and his descendants will inherit it" (Numbers 14:24, emphasis mine). And what happened to the ten spies who bad-mouthed God's promises? They died in a plague, finding the death they had focused on (Numbers 14:28–29, 36–38).

"I Think of Jesus"

Lately, my focus has been drawn to a conflict with a friend. The problem looked bigger than God's promises. Then, God led me to a conversation with Georgia, my twelve-year-old niece. As she began sharing about difficulties in a friendship, I couldn't help but think of my conflict with my friend. It was a cue from God to learn from my niece.

Georgia's heart was hurt, but she didn't seem to carry a heavy burden. I asked her how she went about her day without those heavy feelings.

She said, "I think of Jesus on the cross."

I asked her how Jesus on the cross affected her focus with her friendship issue.

"I think of Jesus crying out, 'Father, forgive them, they know not what they do.' I want to look like Jesus so I'm choosing to pray, 'Father, forgive my friends; they likely don't know how much it hurts me.'"

I took it all in. Georgia prayed for her friend because she understood that if her friend received grace and forgiveness, that friend, too, may be changed by Jesus for the better. Rather than focusing on the pain of the conflict, Georgia focused on the promises of forgiveness and healing. Georgia chose to seek Jesus with all her heart, and you know what she found? Jesus! Jesus will never leave her nor forsake her! Jesus forgives! Jesus is her help! When Georgia focused on Jesus with all her heart, He transformed her heart for her friend. Let's choose to find God in our conflicts, our temptations, and our trials.

"Seek the kingdom of God above all else, and live righteously, and he will give you everything you need" (Matthew 6:33 NLT). We often equate this verse with the cliché, "God won't give you more than you can handle." Let's clarify here—that phrase is not biblical. It's not Scripture. Rather, God *is* in the habit of giving you more than you can handle, so that you rely on His help in the midst of it! God doesn't promise a life without conflict or temptation or trial. Rather, He promises His help in the midst of it all. Georgia had everything she needed while in the conflict with her friend, but not because God immediately solved the problem. In the middle of her own trials, Georgia remembered to focus on not only the promise, but the Promise Giver too.

What Has God Promised?

I don't want to leave you with an inspirational idea without giving you some of the infinite concrete promises found in Scripture. If you need help seeking and finding God, set your heart on some of these promises. The Bible is full of unambiguous promises. Here is a smattering of my favorites:

He promises to give us wisdom if we ask (James 1:5).

He promises to provide a way out of temptation
(1 Corinthians 10:13).

He promises that our salvation is secure, no matter what
(John 10:28–29).

He promises to never leave us nor forsake us (Hebrews
13:5).

He promises to finish the good work He has begun in us
(Philippians 1:6).

He promises to come back (Luke 12:40).

These promises are a sure thing. Notice, though, how they have much more to say about who God is and how He is sanctifying us than about any specific outcome or circumstance. In all of Paul's recorded prayers, he never prayed for circumstances to change. Isn't. That. Interesting? Paul knew to focus all his heart on God and His power, His control, and His promises in Scripture.

Who Is It Today, Lord?

How do we remember God's promises more than the problems? How do we consistently seek God with *all our heart* each day?

Start with a personal heart checkup. I often pray David's prayer from Psalm 139:23–24 (NLT): "Search me, O God, and know my heart; test me and know my anxious thoughts. Point out anything in me that offends you, and lead me along the path of everlasting life." I write out the words "search my heart" and wait. I then write down anything God brings up in my spirit. Join me, write down anything God is finding in your heart. The good, bad, and ugly. Let your ugly lead you to His forgiveness and the good bring you to worship.

Then, encourage others, and let them encourage you. My husband and I text each other one sentence, summarizing what we receive from God by reading His Word each day. It gives us truth to focus on and accountability in seeking God.

Finally, you may choose to seek to live like my friends Sue and Rick Beeney. Years ago, they started asking a question that has since enabled them to seek God each day with all their heart: "Who is it today, Lord?"

It's a prayer. It's a question. It's inspiring, and it's the focus of all their heart each day. Who will we have the opportunity to impact for God's glory today? Will it be a coffee barista? A friend who needs a favor? Each other? This question gives a focus to their day and keeps their eyes on an agenda. And each day, they end up with a great story. As someone who has been a benefactor of their love, I must admit it's effective.

Give God all of your heart; you'll find Him when you do. That's a promise. We are not promised a safe and easy life. We are not promised certainty in our circumstances, but we are promised certainty in the God of our circumstances. He is worthy of "all our heart."

PART 4

"I will be found by you," declares the Lord, "and will bring you back from captivity. I will gather you from all the nations and places where I have banished you," declares the Lord, "and will bring you back to the place from which I carried you into exile."

—Jeremiah 29:14

CHAPTER 11

FREE PEOPLE
FREE PEOPLE

"I will be found by you," declares the L̠ord,
"and **will bring you back from captivity.**
I will gather you from all the nations and
places where I have banished you," declares
the L̠ord, *"and will bring you back to the*
place from which I carried you into exile."

▪ ▪ ▪ ▪ ▪

God doesn't save us from something without
also saving us for something.

L̲ike most teenagers, I toilet papered houses in high school. But, even in pranking, I brought my very best effort. These midnight adventures became an avenue of artistic expression for my friends and me. We themed our lawn décor. Our target—ahem, friend—would discover that someone had tortilla'd their house, and also left chips and salsa. Or we'd set up beach scenery with folding chairs, old beach towels, and broken umbrellas. Other times we'd drop off dozens of empty pizza boxes, stacked in a neat tower on the front doorstep.

At school one day, one of my friends admitted she'd never gotten to "experience the fun" of being toilet papered. I almost felt bad for her. Then she explained that she lived in a gated community. I stopped feeling bad for her, but I knew a challenge when I heard one. I invited my neighbors Colin and Shayla. Remember sailor Colin? Same Colin. Our plan was to roll up to the security guard and say it was our friend's birthday. We would even show him the wrapped present we'd brought for her.

The security guard was skeptical. I figured this was going to happen, so I had planned ahead. I handed him my phone, showing him the contact info for our friend's mom, encouraging him to call her. I had changed the number to Shayla's—and, from her spot hidden in the back of the van, she answered the call. Within a minute the security bar was lifted and off we went to have our fun. We were only halfway through the second bag of tortillas when we got caught.

Thinking back, I bet the security guards enjoyed scaring us far more than we enjoyed our ten minutes of fun. The trick with Shayla's phone hadn't worked. The guards had waited just long enough to chase us off the property and out of the gated community with sirens and lights.

I recently shared this story at brunch with my family. We had guests, and we were going around the table, talking about what we had been like in high school. In the middle of the story my dad, who had heard the story at least a dozen times before, interrupted. "I remember that because I was in the back of the van!"

We all stared at him. He was laughing hysterically, almost falling out of his chair. I asked in disbelief, "You were there?"

"Yeah! I was in the back of the van!" He snorted, and then recited from memory the next details of the story.

Are you confused? Imagine how I felt. Now, I must admit that my memory doesn't always serve me right. There is a slim (and I mean *very* slim) chance my dad was actually in the back of the van. Either way, what resulted was a lot of laughter and a family joke. To this day, when a familiar story is being told, you can feel free to insert yourself into it. The joke makes most stories, especially the familiar ones, a bit more exciting. That afternoon my dad entered into my story. In his retelling, he laughed harder than anyone and built suspense like a true first-person storyteller. That day at brunch, Dad fully entered into my story.

The Author of the Story

God doesn't just enter into our stories, He writes them. God is the author of both our individual stories and His one, grand redemptive story.

Two stories unfold simultaneously in each of our lives. Randy Frazee calls them the lower story and the upper story.[1] The lower story is the one we experience and understand from our five-foot-something perspective, and the upper story is the overarching story that is written and told from God's perspective.

We're all familiar with lower stories. They're the stories that we live every day. Our families, our schools, our jobs, our plans, our dreams, our hobbies, and everything else. Sometimes our lower stories are fun and exciting, sometimes they're mundane and routine, and other times, they're really low. God's people also lived out "lower stories." Noah, for instance, spent forty days in a dark and cramped ark while everything he had ever known was washed away. Joseph was beaten by his jealous brothers; the whole nation of Israel was enslaved to Babylon; and so on.

The fabric of history is made up of lower stories, all the way forward in time to you and me. Just because they're "lower stories" doesn't mean that they're negative or bad. It just means that they are subplots within a much greater story. In fact, knowing this reframes the low moments of our lower stories. It gives us hope that even the dark threads are being woven into a beautiful tapestry. We just have to take a couple of steps back to see the big picture.

In the upper story, God weaves all of those lower stories together into His one good, divine love story. God's power and promises bring Noah to dry ground. God uses the poor choices of those jealous brothers to save an entire nation. God even used Babylon, the evil pagan power, to chastise, refine, and ultimately redeem His people. They went back home, rebuilt their cities, and treasured their Scriptures. One day, a man who was born in Bethlehem could tell them all, "I was here the whole time." He's still trying to convince us of the same thing—"It's Me. Trust Me. I've been here the whole time."

God is writing an incredible story and He's not done yet. He is carefully and thoughtfully weaving billions of stories. Like a good storyteller, He uses character development, conflict, sacrifice, plot twists, climactic scenes, and surprising endings to build His overarching story of redemption.

If we get caught up with the lower stories, even the good

ones, we'll completely miss God's unfolding upper story. God invites us to hold our stories with open hands. With this posture, we can hand our stories over to be used for God's purposes. Whether we let Him or not, He is writing a story through all of history. The question is, will He write His story through us or in spite of us? Will we surrender our stories to Him and so experience the joy of partnership with God, or will we hold tightly to our (lower) stories, unaware of the bigger (upper) picture, and so miss out on the kingdom of God that is literally right in front of us? If you'll let Him, He'll use the worst of your lower stories.

God Pursues His People

God entered into the children of Israel's lower story through Jeremiah's prophecy as he spoke to them, "'I will be found by you,' declares the LORD, 'and **will bring you back from captivity**. I will gather you from all the nations and places where I have banished you,' declares the LORD, 'and will bring you back to the place from which I carried you into exile'" (Jeremiah 29:14).

The people of Israel repeatedly refused to obey the Lord's instructions leading up to this particular (not their first) round of captivity and, yet, God continued to be willing to bless them *if* they repented. He is stubbornly determined to bless his people. But they didn't repent. Jeremiah prophesied that God would judge them for their disobedience by sending them into exile in Babylon. Jeremiah had to live through the horror of his prophecies. Disobedience led to captivity. It still leads to captivity today.

And then we come to Jeremiah chapter 29 verse 14, bringing good news of undeserved freedom. The Lord's words were *to* the Israelites, outlining the specifics of His promised plans *for* them. He said He will be found and the people will be free. In His time, of course. He spoke to them in their painful waiting and reminded them of their specific future.

But why did God choose to speak to them after decades of disobedience? Why now? It's easy to map out ways for God to be more efficient. But we have to remember we're not the Author. We don't see the whole picture. And, yes, from our perspective we might want God to speak differently or sooner or to never allow us to be in a situation like exile in the first place. But, when we take a step back and look at the bigger picture, the upper story, we realize God didn't have to speak to them at all. After everything He had put up with from His stubborn and rebellious people, He would have been justified in writing them off entirely. God didn't speak to them, nor does He speak to us, because we deserve it.

God doesn't play by our rules. He doesn't play by our consequences, either. We deserve to be dismissed, yet God graciously and kindly still chooses to pursue the relationship with an undeserved message of grace and an overarching story of redemption. He comes *to* his people to remind us we were chosen *for* Him.

This Word Is for You

It's difficult to enter into Israel's story, a story that's not about us. The book of Jeremiah was not written *to* us, that's true. But it was written *for* us. This is part of the miracle of Scripture, the living words of God. These words, even the ones that seem obscure or bleak or beyond your comprehension level, are for you. Believe it.

Most of us abandon the "Bible in a year" plan in February because it's easier to put our time, energy, and talents into something—anything—that's directed *to* us. We're more likely to respond to personal text messages than comment on blog posts. We'll read and respond to a handwritten letter *to* us, but we don't send a postcard in response to a citywide announcement.

I wonder if we miss hearing and responding to God's words *for* us because we're waiting to hear what God is saying directly *to* us. We're so busy looking for a personal word from the Lord that we neglect His Word for us. But the fact is, His Word is a word directly to us. The Bible is our story. We may be characters in a different chapter than the exiles in Jeremiah, but we're still a part of the same story. Theologian N. T. Wright refers to God's story as a five-act play.[2] We are living in the fifth act (labeled "The Church"), and in order to live this act well, we need to know what came before. It's all part of the same story. And if our part is a part of the story, that means the God who was working in and through His people, the Israelites, is still working in and through us. The God who led His people through exile to redemption is doing the same in and through us. It means that God is doing more in you than you can see. God is using your life for bigger purposes.

After we surrender our lives to Him and receive salvation, we need to continue to give Him our troubles and our days. We need to place our lower stories in His hands and trust Him for His direction. Those who put everything in God's hands will see God's hand in everything. The Bible was not written *to* us but *for* us to see God and His character and trust Him more with our lives. In reading God's plans *to* the Israelites, we can grow in trust of God's timing for our own freedom.

Freedom is coming! Only God knows when or how. This is as true now as it was then. Will you see the ways He's already entered your story? Will you trust Him?

From Prophetic Word to Present Reality

As far as entering the story goes, my dad was good. But Jesus is better. He knew exactly the part to break into. And He broke in fully. One day Jesus walked into a synagogue, where He was handed the scroll of the prophet Isaiah. He unrolled the scroll and read these words: "The Spirit of the Lord is on me, because he has anointed me to proclaim good news to the poor. He has sent me to proclaim freedom for the prisoners and recovery of sight for the blind, to set the oppressed free, to proclaim the year of the Lord's favor" (Luke 4:18–19). Jesus then rolled up the scroll and declared: "Today this scripture is fulfilled in your hearing" (Luke 4:21).

In that moment good news for the needy, freedom for prisoners, and sight for the blind went from prophetic words to a present reality, from words to flesh and blood. Jesus declared that Isaiah was talking about Him! Jesus was claiming that these words had come to life through Him. It's as if Jesus was insisting, "I was in the back of the van the whole time!" He stepped into the story, and confusion ensued; His audience was both amazed and furious (see Luke 4:22, 28). Like my dad, Jesus was rearranging their whole understanding of the past. But unlike my dad, Jesus was declaring the truth.

Isaiah's prophecy was fulfilled by Jesus himself. Isaiah's words came to life in Jesus's life. Jesus was the One who preached good news, healed the sick, gave sight to the blind, and freed the oppressed.

By putting on flesh and blood, Jesus entered into our story. I like the way Eugene Peterson translated John 1:14: "The Word became flesh and blood, and moved into the neighborhood" (MSG). Because God fully entered in, He fully understands. Have you felt betrayed? Jesus understands. Felt weakness because of temptation? He knew what that was like as well. Have you been misunderstood? Have you felt like God Himself was asking too much of you? Believe it or not, Jesus understands all of this.

He created the story, spoke to His people throughout it, and He also entered into it, fully. Why did He enter into the story? He didn't have to. He chose to. He chose to because He loves us, because He loves the world.

Jesus chose to enter into the story because we had messed it up so badly. Because even after God created perfection, we chose to trust someone else. Maybe it started with Adam and Eve, but the tradition has been carried on ever since. Over and over again, the children of Israel chose to trust other gods, or kings, or their own wisdom. We do the same thing. We have been offered the perfection of God's grace, but we choose to place our trust in our money, or in the opinions of others, or in our perception of our own strength, or beauty, or talent. Does that sound like slavery to you? Because, in practice, anything that's not "trusting God" looks a lot like slavery. Jesus was the promise of freedom for them and is the same promise of freedom for us.

What Is Freedom?

What goes through your mind when you read the word *freedom*? There's that wild feeling you get when you've outrun gated community security guards—that's something like freedom. There's momentary freedom, there is the freedom to speak up, there is the freedom to change. Maybe for you, freedom sounds like a joke or a dream that's too good to be true. That's fair. But there is real freedom, and it is good.

There is both freedom *from* and freedom *to*. We need freedom from every power that would enslave us, that would steal, kill, and destroy the life that God has given us. But it is not just freedom from these things so that we can do whatever we want (the standard definition of freedom). If freedom simply means doing whatever I want, then I've just been set free from one thing only to be enslaved to another, to be enslaved to myself. But God frees us to Himself. He ransoms us to Himself. This is why Paul says we are free *from* sin and slaves *to* righteousness.

Freedom is powerful. But it isn't free. When it comes to your freedom, Jesus bought and paid for it with His life. Listen, again, to what He has to say about it:

> "The Spirit of the Lord is on me, because he has anointed me to proclaim good news to the poor. He has sent me to proclaim freedom for the prisoners and recovery of sight for the blind, to set the oppressed free, to proclaim the year of the Lord's favor."

Jesus was anointed to preach good news. What area of

your life could use good news right now? Think about the most hopeless place you've ever been. Jesus has good news—that hopeless place is not the end of your story.

He proclaims freedom for prisoners. What does your prison look like? Are you stuck in the prison of others' opinions? How about the prison of your own expectations?

He brings recovery of sight for the blind. Where are your blind spots? Have you been able to see Him clearly lately, or is something standing in the way? What makes it hard to see Jesus? What blurs your vision of Him and His work in and through you?

This is the Year of the Lord's favor. Do you know what that means? He wants to free you. He's doing this of His own free will because He loves you so desperately. *And* because He loves everyone you're going to come in contact with. Remember, there is a bigger story being written.

You've probably heard the saying, "Hurt people hurt people." Yes, I'll give you that one. But did you ever hear this one: Healed people heal people. And free people free people! Anything God does *to* you is not meant to stop with you. If the story didn't go from people to others, our Bible would only contain the first three pages. The story continued through His people. He is inviting us to continue His upper story through our lives. He freed you to free others.

Going beyond Ourselves to Reach Others

Our freedom in God's story is not just about us. After we find that freedom, our story is about glorifying God so that others can discover His character through us. In order to show God to others, we must fully enter into their stories. We rarely enter into other people's stories as they tell them. We cordially nod and smile and, at times, celebrate, but it's hard to fully enter in and attempt to feel what they felt. It's difficult to enter into someone else's joy when we're too consumed with finding our own or wondering why they have it and we don't. But Jesus is asking us to go beyond ourselves.

Jesus commissioned us to share the good news of freedom: "Go and make disciples of all nations, baptizing them in the name of the Father and of the Son and of the Holy Spirit, and teaching them to obey everything I have commanded you. And surely I am with you always, to the very end of the age" (Matthew 28:19–20). This Great Commission, as it has come to be known, was given after Jesus died and resurrected but before He ascended into heaven. Yes, there Jesus was— decidedly not dead, and entrusting His disciples with His final words. His presence was proof of His power. Here's the point: Jesus not only gives them a mission, He also gives them the means, the power, to accomplish that mission: His presence.

Again, none of us were there. The Great Commission wasn't said *to* anyone who is reading this book. But it was given *for* us. Jesus has all the authority to commission us to be a part of His work in the world, to be a part of His redemptive story, and His presence will make it possible.

Don't limit God. Get Him out of any box you've placed Him in. And, while we're talking about boxes, get out of the box you've placed yourself in, limiting what God can do through you. Anything God will call you to is possible because the One with all authority will be with you. How do I know? Just look at what happens after the Great Commission. Jesus ascends into heaven, but He sends His Holy Spirit to be with His followers. And that's where the fun begins.

A doctor named Luke wrote both the Gospel of Luke and the book of Acts. In Acts 1:1, Luke says that in his former book (the book of Luke), "I wrote about all that Jesus *began* to do and to teach" (emphasis added). Luke is saying that the book he is currently writing, the book of Acts, tells about what Jesus will *continue* to do. But, wait, didn't Jesus ascend into heaven in the first chapter of Acts? He did. Luke is implying that the book of Acts records what Jesus is *continuing* to do through His disciples . . . which includes us.

What is Jesus up to in your workplace? Well, if Jesus dwells within you by His Spirit, then I can ask, what are *you* up to in your workplace? What you're up to *is* what He is up to. What is Jesus up to in your broken family? Well, what are *you* up to in your broken family? Have you ever witnessed an injustice in the world and shaken your fist at God screaming, "What are you doing about this?" I wonder if God is in heaven thinking, "Well, (insert your name), it looks like I made you pretty passionate about it. What are *you* going to do about it?"

What if what God was doing about the injustices in the world was making us more aware of them? If you're asking, "What is God up to?" follow that up with this question: What are *you* up to? Maybe what you're up to is precisely what He is up to, through you. What you do matters.

We can have hope that God is moving because we are moving. No wonder we call the Christian life "following Jesus." The term *following* only makes sense if our leader is moving. Jesus, the One we're following, is moving. Oh, and we're not alone. He is with us now. And He will be with us forever.

CHAPTER 12

20/20

"I will be found by you," declares the L**ORD**,
"and will bring you back from captivity. **I will
gather you from all the nations and places
where I have banished you,***"* declares the
L**ORD**, *"and will bring you back to the place
from which I carried you into exile."*

• • • • •

Free people free people.

My friend Bob Goff is spectacular.[1] If you've read his
books or heard him speak, you know he's an incredible
communicator, dedicated to helping his audience put into
practice his message of loving everyone, always. As lights
hit the stage of any venue, Bob walks out with his full-sized
smile and says something witty, yet brilliant. He's playful
and amazing and spontaneous. There might be thousands of
people there, but Bob cares about each of them individually.

He doesn't want listeners, he wants collaborators. He wants everyone involved, always. The whole audience leaves more ready to love people, less conscious of their previous excuses to merely focus on themselves.

Shortly after we met, Bob sent me a text-invite to, of all places, Uganda: "Come! You'll flip! Let's go love on some people!" Since my love language is adventure, impromptu is no problem, and the friendship was off to a great start.

Right before we left, friends asked about the itinerary. I didn't know. I never asked Bob about the plans. I trusted that we would do what he said, "love some people." Bob has taught me that daily plans don't need to be more complex than loving people. That mission is effective and transformative. It's precisely what Jesus did.

The reason I'm so impressed by people like Bob is their simple motive to live like Jesus: seeing the needs of others and doing something about it.

His Plans Are Better

So tell me, friend, what's your plan for today? For your life? If you've gotten to this final chapter, I hope you've started rethinking what it means to have a plan. I hope you're holding any plans you make (even the seemingly insignificant ones) with open hands. I hope you are learning to trust God's plans because you know more about His character. Be prepared: He may ask you to opt out of your plans. Remember, His plans are better.

God's plans may not look productive, at least by our standard of productive. Jesus didn't even start His public ministry until the last three years of His life. And even then, after He began His ministry, Jesus confused large crowds, stymied the seemingly spiritual, and transformed the least significant of people: fishermen, adulterous women, and a tiny tax collector, to name a few. Purposeful? Yes. Strategic by human standards? Hardly. God's plans might not make any sense at all to us. After all, did it make sense for the most charismatic, powerful, loving human being ever to have walked the face of the earth to be hung on a cross? But where would we be if Jesus hadn't surrendered Himself to the Father's plan? His plan rarely looks like we think it should, but it is always meant for good. He is always good.

God's plan for you is good, and while I can't tell you all of the specifics, I can give you the big picture. His plan for you is to follow Jesus and become more like Him. His plan is not specifically a place; it's trust in a Person. That's the main goal of His good plan for you. Jesus Himself is the "good" He wants to give you. His main goal has nothing to do with the cultural definitions of good: success, riches, popularity, or recognition. Instead, His plan for your life is simply this: love. Love for God and love for others.

"Love" seems so vague, doesn't it? You don't get a diploma for loving, nor do you get a raise or promotion. Love is not something you'll be able to measure or quantify. Love is not terribly productive or strategic, and other than loving one's spouse and family, love will often make no sense to the people around you. That's what I found so inspiring and transformative about Bob's agenda: "Let's go love on some people!" Love is a goal that goes way beyond any title or honor or reward, and in that way, it's a great mission statement for any follower of Jesus.

With love in mind as a goal, let me ask you, how would today look different if your plan was more about loving people than getting things done? While we could accomplish both, let's prioritize God's plans and let our plans look like His.

The Community Commandment

Remember Jeremiah 29:11 when God said He knows the plans He has for His people? Well, as we've read on and come to verse 14, we're struck by a pretty profound realization: these plans that God has are not just for us. Instead, God has plans for others too. He declares in verse 14: "I will gather you from all the nations and places where I have banished you . . ." Now, what does that mean? That means that God isn't talking to an individual here but to a whole nation, to a community of people. In other words, all of the "yous" in this passage are plural! So often, when we read Jeremiah 29:11, we read with ourselves at the center of the story. We imagine all of the good plans that God has for "me" personally. And when we do that, we miss the fact that God's good plans are always given and lived out in community. His good plans are not for "me" but are for "us."

When God says, "I will gather you," He is inviting us beyond our individualism and egocentrism and into a deeper understanding of His heart for community. Trusting God means yielding our own plans, expectations, and ideas of good so we can learn the joy of gathering with others. Because when we let go of our plans, when we declare that we trust Him, there is finally room in our lives for the people around us. For all of our neighbors, near and far.

The beauty of community is this: in community, we can

truly meet the needs of others. And we can have our own needs met in ways that aren't quick fixes, that aren't shallow or temporary. The next time you wish God would use some kind of magic to fix or rearrange your life, remember this: God's response to our needs often involves our friends and families. Instead of time machines or winning lottery tickets, God gives us each other.

Remember the mat bearers (Mark 2:1–12)? The guys who were holding a paralyzed man and lowered him to Jesus through the roof of an actual house? Talk about friendship. When you don't have courage to call on the Lord and doubt that He will heal you, look to the corners of your mat. Make sure you have friends there. Make sure you have friends close enough to touch the very thing you're resting on for safety. Make sure you have faith-filled friends who will bring you to Jesus. Who are your mat bearers? Soon enough, it's going to be your turn to hold the mat.

God gathers us together and uses us for each other. Like the blind man in John 9. He receives his sight instantly, but what he most needs is faith. Over the course of the chapter, his faith grows and becomes unshakeable as he has conversations . . . with other *people*. Miracles produce community. In fact, the end result of Jesus's miracles is the restoration of community. The demon-possessed guy in Mark 5 is sent back to his community, the bleeding woman is restored to her community, parents receive their children back from the dead, and the Samaritan woman runs back into the town to the people she has been hiding from and gets to be a part of the community again (Mark 5:1–17; 5:25–34; 5:41; John 4:29).

I love this! Miracles really do produce community! Think

about that the next time you're in a rough spot—maybe this is the context that God will use to deepen your experience of community.

Glasses in Uganda

Speaking of God's glory shining through brokenness and difficult circumstances, let me tell you how the rest of that trip with Bob turned out. I started off each morning in Uganda seeking and finding God's character through a chapter-a-day in the book of John. Because Jesus is unchanging, I was confident that who Jesus was then is still true of Him today. In those chapters, I read that He is loving and fearless, that He is much more interested in people than in pat answers, and He wants me to know Him. Each morning, I told Him I wanted to see Him. That I needed help seeing Him. I asked Him for help to look like Him, to do what He would do in this particular place and time. I prayed for the real "good" of Christlikeness. This routine made it possible for me to love others, rather than loving the idea of Megan Marshman loving others. After remembering the character of Christ and receiving His love and attention, I felt prepared to pour Him out. Seen by Him, I was ready to truly see Him in others.

One morning, we visited one of the schools Bob and his wife Maria had built, and we were told that we would be opening up the school's first library. That morning was the first I'd heard of this, and I flipped. Not only would the students get to pick up new books, they would also get to pick out a new pair of prescription glasses! I was floored by the thoroughness of this plan. Books are nice, but they're only going to change someone's life if they can be read.

The glasses had been delivered and numbered so each student could be matched with the right prescription. Bob's wife Maria and I laid out the glasses in prescription order and the adventure began.

The first student in line had his eyes tested for a prescription before getting the chance to walk through the library to grab a book. This was the plan for each of the kids—they'd take an eye test, grab a book, and then come back to the table to receive their new glasses. That first student made his way through the rows of books with utter amazement. He couldn't believe they were all now available to him. After some deliberation, he chose a book, and made his way to our table full of glasses. He handed me a slip of paper with his name and the number of his prescription. I handed him a pair of glasses with a +1.0 sticker. He tried them on as he glanced down at the book. Simultaneously, his eyes widened and his jaw dropped. He looked up at me in amazement. He peered back down at the book. With one hand, he pulled the glasses off, looked at the cover, and then slowly pulled them back up. It was like he wanted to make sure the miracle was a permanent one. I smiled. So did he. *It worked!*

He started to wander away, staring down at his book, but I stopped him. I didn't want him to miss out on the next step. I gestured to a line of varying shapes, styles, and colors of glasses and told the young boy with excitement, "Now you get to pick out your style."

The kid looked at me quizzically. "Style?"

"Yes, style!" I put one hand on my hip and awkwardly dipped to the side. I reminded myself that some of these students were still learning the English language and noted that the word *style* wasn't a priority. *How interesting.*

Kid after kid walked up to our table, tried on a new pair of glasses, glanced at a book in amazement, and looked back at us as if we were Jesus Himself—bringing sight to the blind. One kid was so mesmerized by the glasses that we couldn't move him away from our table. I eventually asked him, "Have you ever worn a pair of glasses before?"

Turning the glasses over in his hand, he shook his head. "Never ever."

It was as if these students had no idea that seeing clearly was even "a thing," let alone an option for them. And that's why we went. To be embedded in the community of God's love, and, in His power, to reveal something totally new.

Did you know that seeing life more clearly is an option for you? Now, of course, I'm not talking about glasses. But you better believe I'm referring to your perspective.

How do you handle hardships? If you're anything like me, there are times when you simply can't see beyond them. That place, that "this is impossible and I'll never survive" place, is where He can come in and make a big difference in your perspective. Do you want to see your own life differently? Well, first of all, tell God you're having trouble seeing Him. Ask for the ability to trust Him. Then look at your circumstances through the lens of God's grace, power, and abiding love for you. What do you see differently when you look through that lens?

Mirrors versus Lenses

At the beginning of our day at the library in Uganda, I was more excited about the students getting to choose a style than the fact that they were gaining eyesight. I figured they would care more about "how they looked" than "what they could now see." We had many different styles, but because the kids couldn't see themselves wearing them, they didn't really discriminate between the pairs. So we sent someone to grab a mirror.

Soon the Ugandan teens began crowding around the mirror. The girls I had pegged as shy came to life as they grabbed two or three pairs of glasses and pushed and shoved their way to model poses in front of the mirror. It was entertaining . . . until it became chaotic.

The system had worked beautifully . . . until the mirror. The line started backing up. The students started to get pickier and even a bit pushy due to the attention they wanted to give their "style." One student tried on one pair, then a different pair, then the first again, then the other. The kids were crowding each other trying to see themselves. Everything slowed down.

Our agenda—love people—had been clear until we brought in the mirror. Because what does the mirror direct your focus to? Mirrors draw our attention to ourselves.

Finally, we got through the line. And the lasting impression the students had was clear sight. Despite the fumbles with the mirror, the students ultimately appreciated the lens more than the mirror.

Here's my takeaway: we will always miss our purpose if we are merely looking at ourselves. Even in the midst of your own needs, which you do have, God invites you to see the needs of others. That's the way He's going to heal your needs: by planting you in community, thereby creating more ways and circumstances for you to trust Him. That's His plan. He saw your needs, met them in Christ, and then turns you to look outward—not at yourself—and see the needs of others.

We need the same thing those students needed—not a mirror, but a lens. Not something that helps us focus more on ourselves, like social media platforms, but a lens that corrects our focus so we can see others more clearly. Jesus is that lens. As we spend time with Him, we begin to see the world (and our lives) as He sees it. We see the world through Him. He gives us glimpses of His kingdom bursting into reality in the lives of the people around us and gives us an opportunity to join Him in that process.

A Community of Participants

During my freshman year of high school, I was quickly losing interest in church. Instead of digging into Bible study, which I had always loved, I stopped responding to the deeper questions from my small group leader. Everything about my posture said, "Whatever."

My youth pastor noticed my attitude. But rather than taking me on a guilt trip, one day he pulled me aside. "Hey," he said. "I've noticed something about you. You really know how to relate to people. So I was wondering, how would you like to be the youth group's 'Initiator of First Impressions'?"

"Wow!" I thought. "That sounds important! I'll try it out!"

I valued my title because I felt significant, unique, known, and empowered to be the best "Initiator of First Impressions" there ever was. Now that I work at a church, I know my title was a fancy synonym for "Greeter." All the same, my youth pastor had invited me to lead, and that opportunity made church feel like it was in some way mine. He assured me that I had something to contribute, but he gave me something I needed even more: the opportunity to actually contribute.

In Ephesians 4, Paul explained that Jesus gave ministerial gifts (apostles, prophets, teachers, evangelists) in order "to equip his people for works of service" (Ephesians 4:12), but in many churches, we have defaulted to "entertaining His people with works of service." Churches have become places where God's people come to watch other people do ministry. We often act as a community of observers when we are called and commissioned to be a community of participants, a community of owners.

The conversation with my youth pastor had a ripple effect in my life. Not only did I become an active participant in the church that year, I also started a Bible study on my high school campus. I became not just a participant in a community, but an owner.

Serving the Local Church

One of my favorite ways to build a God-honoring, transformational community is to serve my local church. Remember, this wasn't always the case for me. For far too long, I saw church as a chore. But then my youth pastor invited me to stop observing and start participating. He invited me to become an owner in my church, and I've loved it ever since.

I love the church! I love it not simply for the ways it can serve me but for the ways I'm invited to serve it. It's not perfect because it's made up of people just like me. It was created to function with contributors, not consumers. Part of my job as a church employee is to make sure people understand this. So one night I decided I needed to teach the young adults to contribute to the church. But instead of just telling them, "you need to contribute," I forced them into it. You see, I decided to throw a potluck! Sure, I'd still give them a message, but I didn't want them to come simply to receive. I wanted them to *bring* something for each other too. And they showed up. That's the strange thing about inviting people to contribute instead of promising to entertain them—they show up. They show up ready to work instead of ready to judge. And they feel like they're a part of something. That's what happened that night.

They showed up not as observers or consumers but as participants, as owners of the best potluck ever. They showed up with fruit and salad, with pizza and casserole and more types of chips and salsa than you can imagine. The only thing missing? Forks! Ha!

And that's the way it is in church too. If you don't bring what's in your hands to bring, the whole church goes without. God has created you very purposefully. He has given you gifts that He wants you to use in your church, and if you don't bring them for any reason (fear, comparison, or apathy, for example), the whole community is worse off for it.

You, dear reader, are invited to contribute precisely how God made you to. You're invited to listen to God's voice and respond in community with His people at your local church. Because when God gathers His people, good things happen. We are released from captivity to sin. We find God. And together, we will begin to see His beautiful kingdom right here on earth. Join in! You'll flip! Let's go love on some people!

THE REST OF THE STORY

Do you trust Him? If the answer is yes, don't just say it, show it. If you're really serious about this "yes," further it by sharing it with others. You won't be the first. Here's what happened after Jeremiah 29:11–14:

About seventy years after the Babylonians conquered Jerusalem and took God's people into exile, Babylon was itself conquered by the Persians.[1] Esther, a Jewish orphan, born in exile in Babylon, was chosen by the Persian emperor to become queen of Persia, and God used her to save His people from death. Around the same time, Nehemiah, a Jewish cupbearer for the Persian king, returned to Israel to rebuild Jerusalem's walls. The Persian king not only let this happen, but he paid for it! This building project was one of the greatest construction projects of the ancient world and was completed in just forty-nine days. Yes, it took only forty-nine days, amidst opposition and unrest in the country. The lineage of the promised Messiah once again resided in their Promised Land of Israel, and the Old Testament came to a close.

For the next four hundred years, something strange happened. God was silent. He didn't speak through a prophet, priest, or king. This is what took place between the Old Testament and New Testament pages in the Bible. The promise of freedom was alive, but hidden, shrouded in God's inexplicable silence. For four hundred years, the people waited for the promise to be revealed.

The Promise Arrives at Last

The Gospel of Matthew opens with a lineage that shows us that God stayed committed to His promise. And at the perfect time in history, the Redeemer arrived in the little town of Bethlehem.

Jesus, the Messiah, was born. He was born to a virgin and raised in the town of Nazareth, just as had been foretold. After spending thirty years working in the family business, Jesus started His public ministry. He called His first disciples and invited them to walk with Him as He shared good news with the poor, set captives free, and gave sight to the blind, just like He said He would. He lived and proclaimed God's kingdom, demonstrated His power, and taught us all a radical new way to live.

He lived as a blameless man—the only one in history. He was the spotless Lamb of God, the perfect sacrifice to pay the price for our sin. God had commanded the Jews in the Law of Moses to practice animal sacrifice as a way of making atonement for their sins. They offered pure, spotless lambs for sins committed against Him. But, as Hebrews 10:4 points out, "It is impossible for the blood of bulls and goats to take away sins."

So God sent Jesus to become the once-and-for-all sacrifice who gives every man, woman, and child access to relationship with God for all time. He was the final sacrificial Lamb of God, and in His crucifixion satisfied God's justice for all time, for all those who accept it. His death paved the road to forgiveness.

But, of course, Jesus didn't stay dead. He didn't come simply to free us from sin but also to free us from sin's companion, death. His resurrection cleared the way for victory over death, so that we who follow Him can also follow Him into new life. And then, He ascended into heaven in order to send us the Holy Spirit to abide in us and to help us to live out in the church community the message of salvation. Empowered by the Holy Spirit, the church, this hodge-podge collection of people, went on to change the world. They preached the gospel across Jerusalem, Judea, and Samaria, and over the millennia since, the message has reached across the earth. People kept saying "yes" to Jesus and it continued through the first disciples who passed it on to others for generations upon generations upon generations . . .

Thousands of years later, a teenager named Jenny said "yes" to Jesus for the first time. She started experiencing a new kind of freedom—she wanted to live for more than herself, she wanted to follow Jesus. This newfound freedom led her to volunteer in children's ministries at her church. In her own words, "I heard that something was developing for kids to learn about God, something I wished I had when I was a kid, so I decided to get involved for the sake of others."

Each week, she showed up at her church to help out with this new Awana program. One Wednesday evening, a leader shared the good news of Jesus Christ, inviting any of the children to come and speak with one of the volunteers if they wanted to know more. After the message, lots of little five- and six-year-old hands went up to talk through what it would mean to give their entire lives over to the lordship of Jesus. I'm sure Jenny felt more comfortable in the back. But when the leader asked her to go sit with this little one in the red vest, Jenny said "yes." She sat with the blonde five-year-old and walked her through a simple message. And the little one said "yes" too.

I was that little girl. I'm following Jenny's lead by saying "yes" to sharing these words with you, dear reader. And now it's your time.

God is gathering people together in His upper story; He has already placed them in your life. He has a plan for them too. My guess is that, for them, He plans to use you. If you'll let Him. Will you say "yes"?

He's Coming Back!

This story won't end with your answer, though. It continues beyond our lives here on earth.

Jesus will return. He will return completely unveiled in all of His glory. He will ride in victory on a white horse to proclaim that He is King of Kings and Lord of Lords forever.

He will judge the nations, and He will eventually send Satan and his followers to suffering and separation. Those who love God and who have accepted His Son, Jesus, will live with Him in the new heaven and new earth forever, in relationship with God—the way it all began in the garden. The way it *should* be. And from that day on, for all of eternity, we will be with the promised Lord and Redeemer forever and ever. Amen!

Dear reader, do you trust him? Who told you to trust Him in the first place? And who will you pass this message on to next?

Don't just say that you trust Him; show your trust with your one wild and precious life. Trust. It's simple yet powerful.

You live your life the way you live your days. Who you choose to trust today matters. Anything that happens to you is never meant to stop with you. Think back to that one long story that started in the beginning. It has been passed down through all those generations and now, it's your turn. God's plan for others involves you. Every lesson you learn is not meant to stop with you; it's meant to go through you and into the life of another.

God has plans for you, and they will include trials. But the plans are still meant for good. His plans invite us into deeper personal intimacy with the God who holds the plans in His hands. This God cares enough to pay attention to us as we pay attention to Him. He listens. And He makes promises He always keeps, such as the one I want you to remember as you move on past this book and into the rest of your life. If you seek Him, you won't be disappointed. He'll free you, speak to you, and gather you with others, all for His glory. He has plans for everyone, and you'll be a part of His plans for others. Don't miss out. Seek God and find Him. He's not hiding, but He sure is inviting. He is inviting you to share what you have found in Him because of a promise He made back in Babylon to His people that if they (and you) seek Him with all your heart, you'll find Him. And God always keeps His promises.

ACKNOWLEDGMENTS

I thank God for tossing people in my path to offer wisdom and encouragement as I follow Jesus.

I am courageous enough to risk and dream and swing for the fences because of the support of my family.

Alex Field, my agent, thank you for initiating the movement of this content from my head to Word docs.

Josh Harrison, you are masterful at organizing ideas and crafting beautiful words. The future of the church will benefit from your voice and leadership.

Meredith Hinds, I'm grateful for your talent, wit, and partnership in whipping this manuscript into shape.

Lori Vanden Bosch—you're a pro.

Carolyn McCready, Sara Riemersma, and the Zondervan team—thanks for uniting with me for the glory of God and good of His church.

NOTES

Chapter 1: Vow of Silence

1. And any of us who consider ourselves leaders and teachers need to be reminded to point our students, whoever they may be, back to the real Expert and Author of their lives.
2. "Socratic Method," Wikipedia, https://en.wikipedia.org/wiki /Socratic_method.
3. These stats are found throughout this book by Martin B. Copenhaver, *Jesus Is the Question* (Nashville: Abingdon Press, 2014).
4. I found this date on the Insight for Living Ministries website (www.insight.org), which is a wonderful collection of many of Charles Swindoll's sermons and teaching materials. "Jeremiah," *Insight for Living Ministries*, https://www.insight .org/resources/bible/the-major-prophets/jeremiah.
5. Jessie Minassian taught me God's definition of *good* during a seminar entitled "3 Ways to Love your Family (Even When They're Hard to Love!)," April 14, 2018, Hume, CA, Hume Lake Christian Camps.

Chapter 2: Not Enough Is Enough

1. The story of Jesus's grief over the death of his friend Lazarus is found in John 11.
2. Matthew 14:13–21; Mark 6:30–44; Luke 9:10–17; John 6:1–15.
3. You can read about Bill Gaultiere's conversation with Dallas Willard back in 2007 here: https://soulshepherding.org/dallas -willards-one-word-for-Jesus/.
4. Just a few examples: Mark 1:43–44, Matthew 9:30.
5. This quote is found in her book, Mother Teresa, *My Life for the Poor* (New York: Ballantine Books, 1987), 98.
6. I think of the man who lies helpless at the pool of Bethesda (John 5:7) and the centurion who begs for the life of his servant (Matthew 8:7). Jesus continually responds to desperation, and He'll respond to ours too.

Chapter 3: Tuesdays with Jesus

1. Rich Ferreria was the first person I ever heard share stories from spending time with an imaginary Jesus. Thanks for the life-changing idea, friend.
2. Jesus shows up at a Pharisee party and calls the host out on not inviting the poor (Luke 14:12–14). He also shows up at the parties of tax collectors and sinners (Mark 2:13–17). And who could forget that wedding at Cana where he turned water to wine (John 2:1–11)?
3. Read those final three chapters of 2 Kings for the rest of the story about the bad kings and inevitable exile.
4. See James 5:16, Mark 6:31, Matthew 6:6, Hebrews 10:25.

Chapter 4: Don't Stop Dreaming

1. Helen Keller wrote this in her book *Optimism*, which was originally published in 1903.
2. You can find the text of Dr. King's whole speech in the

national archives website: *National Archives*, The US National Archives and Records Administration, https://www.archives .gov/files/press/exhibits/dream-speech.pdf.

3. Are you a student? Do you have a student? Do you know anyone who might fall into that category? Let me be the first to point you to their website . . . https://www.slulead.com/.

4. Commentators are divided on what this verse means. It either means God's inheritance or ours (the inheritance that God is bestowing on us). There is certainly precedent in the Old Testament that God's people are His inheritance . . . see next footnote.

5. But here's my case: God calls us His inheritance. Over, and over, and over again . . . we are His inheritance. Deuteronomy 4:20, 9:26; 1 Samuel 10:1; 1 Kings 8:51, 53; Psalm 28:9, 33:12, 74:2, 78:62, 78:71, 79:1, 94:14, 106:5, 106:40; Isaiah 19:25, 63:17; Jeremiah 10:16, 16:18, 51:19; Zechariah 2:12.

Chapter 5: Who before What

1. J. I. Packer, *Knowing God*, twentieth anniversary ed. (Westmont, IL: InterVarsity, 1993), 42.

2. Job 34:14–15: If it were His intention and He withdrew His spirit and breath, all humanity would perish together and mankind would return to the dust.

3. C. S. Lewis, *Mere Christianity* (New York: HarperCollins, 1980), 168.

4. Mike@MikeFoster2000. (Instagram, September 23, 2019). Retrieved from https://www.instagram.com/p/B2xzSN _jER6/.

5. If you've never been to Narnia, start with C. S. Lewis, *The Lion, the Witch, and the Wardrobe* (New York: HarperCollins, 2002), 81. The book was originally published in 1950.

Chapter 6: The Man without a Home

1. Jesus asks His followers to carry crosses in these verses: Matthew 10:38, 16:24; Mark 8:34; Luke 9:23, 14:27.
2. James Bales, *The Hub of the Bible—Or—Acts Two Analyzed* (Shreveport, LA: Lambert Book House, 1960), 81–82.
3. You can read the whole sermon here: "Calling on His Name," *The Old Paths Archive*, http://www.oldpaths.com/Archive /Brown/T/Pierce/1923/calling.html.
4. Illustration adapted from a sermon by Andy Cook entitled "Created to Bear Fruit" (Lifeway, 2004).
5. C. S. Lewis, *The Weight of Glory*, reprint ed. (New York: HarperOne, 2001), 32.

Chapter 7: Lord, Teach Us to Pray

1. John Piper@JohnPiper, Twitter, October 20, 2009, 2:02 p.m.
2. Walter Brueggemann, *Praying the Psalms: Engaging Scripture and the Life of the Spirit*, 2nd ed. (Eugene, OR: Wipf and Stock, 2007), 44.
3. Dr. John Coe delivered a message at a young adult pastor's conference entitled "Dark Night of the Soul," April 30, 2019, Lake Forest, CA, Saddleback Church.
4. This concept was adapted from an interview with Dallas Willard on his personal daily practices. See https://www .youtube.com/watch?v=GqLmeubS65Q.
5. And while Paul wrote Colossians, Ephesians, Philippians, and Philemon, he was in prison!
6. Mike Foster@MikeFoster2000. (March 26, 2019). https:// www.instagram.com/p/BvecwDfjkEq/.
7. Max Lucado, *The Great House of God* (Nashville, TN: Thomas Nelson, 2011), 81.
8. Ibid.
9. Timothy Keller, *Prayer* (London: Penguin Books, 2016), 238.

Chapter 8: Amazing Byproduct, Terrible Goal

1. John Ortberg has a great book, *Who Is This Man?: The Unpredictable Impact of the Inescapable Jesus* (Grand Rapids, MI: Zondervan, 2014) that talks about the impact of Jesus on the whole world (not just the church). What's fascinating is that so many Christians are apprehensive about sharing their faith, but many non-Christians would welcome a conversation about Jesus.

2. We often settle for so much less than God. Our problem is that we have gotten the order wrong: we seek first to know ourselves, and then use God to help us realize what we think we have discovered about ourselves. The biblical order is just the opposite: know God first, and then you have the capacity to know yourself. And this makes sense when you think about it. Paul's life changed when he asked the question, "Who are you, Lord?" Receiving the answer to that question freed him up to discover who he was created to be.

3. J. P. Moreland shares about happiness being an amazing byproduct but a terrible goal in his book. J. P. Moreland, *Lost Virtue of Happiness: Discovering the Disciplines of the Good Life* (Colorado Springs, CO: NavPress, 2006).

4. I've stumbled across far too many lesson plans inviting us to "become more like David" when studying his fight with Goliath. Was David brave? Yes! Do we want to be brave? Of course. But do we want to become more like David? Well, only if we stop reading his life story after Goliath. The goal of David and Goliath is not to become more like David but to see Jesus as victorious. In the story, we're not meant to find ourselves as David, but as the hiding Israelites. The need = the hiding/fearful Israelites = ultimately, us. The enemy = Goliath = ultimately, sin and its consequences. The challenge: defeat him = ultimately, defeat sin. On your own you can't fix

yourself and your own sin and its consequences. You need a Savior to fight the battle you've already failed.

5. Rick Warren, *The Purpose Driven Life* (Grand Rapids, MI: Zondervan, 2002).

6. I love that old analogy when it comes to managing our time: you've got a bucket of some big rocks, small rocks, pebbles, and sand. If you start by putting in the sand and the pebbles, you'll never fit everything in the bucket. But if you put the big rocks in first, then the small rocks, then the pebbles, then the sand, you'll find that there's room for everything.

7. Check out the Tullian Tchividjian book, *Jesus + Nothing = Everything* (Wheaton, IL: Crossway, 2011).

8. Check out John Piper's *God Is the Gospel* (Wheaton, IL: Crossway, 2005).

Chapter 9: How's My Driving?

1. This first story was originally published in New Life Church's blog, *HomeFront Magazine*, https://homefrontmag.com /hows-my-driving/.

2. You can find this same pattern—blessed, then told to act—in Romans. Paul passionately urges us in Romans 12 to live our life as a living sacrifice and to not conform to the pattern of the world, but only because he spent eleven chapters outlining what Christ has already done. This is why Romans 12 begins "in view of God's mercy." In other words, in view of chapters 1 through 11, now live in response. Live differently. Because you're already found "in Him," now live like Him.

Chapter 11: Free People Free People

1. Check out Frazee's book, *The Heart of the Story: God's Masterful Design to Restore His People* (Grand Rapids, MI: Zondervan, 2011).

2. The essay in which N. T. Wright explores this idea was

originally published in the journal *Vox Evangelica* in 1991, but is available also here: http://ntwrightpage.com/2016/07/12/how-can-the-bible-be-authoritative/.

Chapter 12: 20/20

1. Get involved! Love on some people! Start at bobgoff.com.

Conclusion: The Rest of the Story

1. The content from God's Grand Redemptive Narrative was originally published in my first book coauthored with Dr. Michelle Anthony, *7 Family Ministry Essentials: A Strategy for Culture Change in Children's and Student Ministries* (Colorado Springs, CO: David C. Cook, 2015), 147.

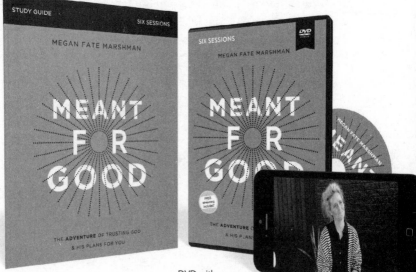